Microsoft Dynamics AX 2012 Services

Effectively use services with Dynamics AX 2012 and create your own services

Klaas Deforche

Kenny Saelen

[PACKT] enterprise
professional expertise distilled
PUBLISHING

BIRMINGHAM - MUMBAI

Microsoft Dynamics AX 2012 Services

First published: December 2012

Production Reference: 1181212

Published by Packt Publishing Ltd.
Livery Place
35 Livery Street
Birmingham B3 2PB, UK.

ISBN 978-1-84968-754-6

www.packtpub.com

Cover Image by Artie Ng (artherng@yahoo.com.au)

Credits

Authors
Klaas Deforche

Kenny Saelen

Reviewers
Palle Agermark

José Antonio Estevan

Tom Van Dyck

Acquisition Editor
Mary Jasmine Nadar

Commissioning Editor
Meeta Rajani

Technical Editors
Manmeet Singh Vasir

Dominic Pereira

Project Coordinator
Shraddha Bagadia

Proofreaders
Aaron Nash

Stephen Silk

Indexer
Hemangini Bari

Graphics
Valentina D'silva

Aditi Gajjar

Production Coordinator
Prachali Bhiwandkar

Cover Work
Prachali Bhiwandkar

About the Authors

Klaas Deforche started working as a developer on Microsoft Dynamics AX in 2007 for the Belgian ICT company RealDolmen, primarily working with Dynamics AX 4.0. He gained experience with AX 2009 while working on projects for some well-known Belgian fashion retailers, especially on the integration side of things. He is currently working on AX 2012 projects for customers in the healthcare sector. Klaas likes to share his knowledge with the community, which is why in 2009 he started his AX-oriented blog `artofcreation.be`.

I would like to thank everyone involved in the making of this book; coauthor Kenny, everyone at Packt Publishing for the opportunity they have given us, and especially the reviewers for their efforts.

Also, I want to acknowledge that writing a book is really hard, not just for the author, but also for the people around them. I always thought that authors were overdoing their thanking, but I can assure you it's quite the opposite. In that respect, thanks to my family, colleagues, friends, and girlfriend for their patience and support.

Also, a big thanks to the readers of my blog, fellow bloggers, and the Dynamics community.

Kenny Saelen works for the Belgian ICT company RealDolmen. He started as a developer on Microsoft Dynamics AX in 2004 primarily working on a European customer implementation with Dynamics AX 3.0. At RealDolmen, he gained experience with Dynamics AX 2009 while implementing AX internally, followed by a project for a books wholesale company. Currently, he is working as a technical architect for a worldwide customer implementation with Microsoft Dynamics AX 2012, mainly working towards integrating Dynamics AX with other technologies such as Sharepoint, Biztalk, and AgilePoint. He can be reached through his blog `ksaelen.be`.

I would like to thank everyone involved in making this book happen, starting with my coauthor Klaas for all the hours we've spent together writing it. Many thanks to everyone at Packt Publishing for the opportunity they have given us, and to the technical reviewers for providing us with the right alternative insights.

Special thanks to my girlfriend and my little son. Writing this book has proven to be much harder than I initially thought, but they have been patiently supporting me all the way.

About the Reviewers

Palle Agermark has spent nearly 20 years in the ERP industry, specializing in Microsoft Dynamics AX, and before that was released in 1998, its predecessor Concorde XAL. Palle has worked for many years at Microsoft Development Center Copenhagen in Denmark, primarily with development on the financial, accounts payable, and accounts receivable modules.

In 2006, Palle wrote the chapter *Extending Microsoft Dynamics AX* in *Inside Microsoft Dynamics AX 4.0, Microsoft Press*.

Currently, Palle works for one of Denmark's largest Microsoft Dynamics AX partners; Logica, now part of CGI.

Palle lives in Denmark, in the Copenhagen area, with his wife Rikke and daughter Andrea.

José Antonio Estevan has been a technical consultant and developer on Dynamics AX since 2008. He has more than 10 years of experience in software development, the last 6 on Dynamics AX since version 4.0. José Antonio is certified in Dynamics AX 2009 and 2012, and has worked on many projects in different sectors with very different requirements, delivering solutions in the form of new developments and integration with all kind of external systems. He has recently been awarded the MVP award from Microsoft.

José Antonio is from Alicante, Spain, but is now living and working in Madrid. He likes to read books, ride his motorbike, and write for the Dynamics AX community on his blog www.jaestevan.com.

Tom Van Dyck is a software engineer and technical consultant for Dynamics AX and currently works for a Microsoft partner in Belgium.

After completing a degree in Computer Science and a few years of Visual Basic, ASP, and SQL programming, he began working with AX in 2004.

Being part of different project teams building a variety of solutions based on AX versions 3.0, 4.0, 2009, and 2012, he has built up a wide practical experience.

Tom is a certified professional for AX with expertise in X++ development, and has a special interest in performance issues and optimization.

I've had the privilege to work with both Kenny and Klaas, and know them as devoted and experienced professionals.

To me this book confirms what I already knew; these guys have a well-thought-out opinion that deserves to be heard. My sincere congrats for the effort and passion they've put into the writing of this book!

www.PacktPub.com

Support files, eBooks, discount offers and more

You might want to visit www.PacktPub.com for support files and downloads related to your book.

Did you know that Packt offers eBook versions of every book published, with PDF and ePub files available? You can upgrade to the eBook version at www.PacktPub.com and as a print book customer, you are entitled to a discount on the eBook copy. Get in touch with us at service@packtpub.com for more details.

At www.PacktPub.com, you can also read a collection of free technical articles, sign up for a range of free newsletters and receive exclusive discounts and offers on Packt books and eBooks.

http://PacktLib.PacktPub.com

Do you need instant solutions to your IT questions? PacktLib is Packt's online digital book library. Here, you can access, read and search across Packt's entire library of books.

Why Subscribe?

- Fully searchable across every book published by Packt
- Copy and paste, print and bookmark content
- On demand and accessible via web browser

Free Access for Packt account holders

If you have an account with Packt at www.PacktPub.com, you can use this to access PacktLib today and view nine entirely free books. Simply use your login credentials for immediate access.

Instant Updates on New Packt Books

Get notified! Find out when new books are published by following @PacktEnterprise on Twitter, or the *Packt Enterprise* Facebook page.

Table of Contents

Preface

Since an ERP system like Microsoft Dynamics AX 2012 plays such a central role in an organization, there will always be the need to integrate it with other applications. In many cases, services are the preferred way of doing this, and Microsoft Dynamics AX 2012 is now more flexible than ever when it comes to the creation and use of these services. Understanding these services will help you identify where they can be used, and do so effectively.

Microsoft Dynamics AX 2012 Services is a hands-on guide that provides you with all of the knowledge you will need to implement services with Microsoft Dynamics AX 2012. The step-by-step examples will walk you through many of the tasks you need to perform frequently when creating and using services.

What this book covers

Chapter 1, Getting Started with Microsoft Dynamics AX 2012 Services, introduces the concept of services and explores the new features and enhancements made to them in Microsoft Dynamics AX 2012.

Chapter 2, Service Architecture and Deployment, dives deeper into the service architecture and explores the different options that are available when deploying services.

Chapter 3, AIF Document Services, focuses on the creation, deployment, and consumption of AIF document services.

Chapter 4, Custom Services, will show you how to create and deploy custom services and consume them using a WCF application using new concepts such as attributes.

Chapter 5, The SysOperation Framework, builds upon the knowledge gained from developing custom services to demonstrate how you can run business logic in Microsoft Dynamics AX 2012 using services and the SysOperation framework.

Chapter 6, Web Services, walks you through the steps needed to consume an external web service in Microsoft Dynamics AX 2012 using Visual Studio integration.

Chapter 7, System Services, demonstrates how powerful system services that are provided out-of-the-box can be, and how they allow you to build applications faster.

What you need for this book

To use the example code files provided with this book, the following prerequisites must be available.

- Microsoft Visual Studio 2010
- Microsoft Dynamics AX 2012
- Microsoft Dynamics AX 2012 Management Utilities

A full list of software requirements can be found in the *Microsoft Dynamics AX 2012 System Requirements* document available for download at `http://www.microsoft.com/en-us/download/details.aspx?id=11094`.

Who this book is for

When you are developing for Microsoft Dynamics AX 2012, you will certainly come into contact with services, even outside of integration scenarios. Because of that, this book is aimed at all Microsoft Dynamics AX developers, both new and those experienced with services and Microsoft Dynamics AX 2012.

This book assumes no other knowledge than a basic understanding of MorphX and X++. Even beginners will be able to understand and complete the examples in this book. Those new to services will get the most out of this book by doing a complete read-through, but those who are experienced can jump right in. The idea is that this book can be used both to educate yourself and as a resource that can be consulted during development.

Some examples use C#.NET, so experience with Visual Studio is a plus but not a must. This book is not aimed at .NET developers.

Conventions

In this book, you will find a number of styles of text that distinguish between different kinds of information. Here are some examples of these styles, and an explanation of their meaning.

Code words in text are shown as follows: "The service contract is a reflection of the DocumentHandlingService class that can be found in the AOT."

A block of code is set as follows:

```
public static void main(Args args)
{
    SysOperationServiceController controller;

    controller = new SysOperationServiceController();
    controller.initializeFromArgs(args);
    controller.startOperation();
}
```

Any command-line input or output is written as follows:

```
T-000505 The Dark Knight 119
T-000506 The Lord of the Rings: The Return of the King 112
```

New terms and **important words** are shown in bold. Words that you see on the screen, in menus or dialog boxes for example, appear in the text like this: "Go to the **Service Groups** node, right-click on it, and click on **New Service Group**."

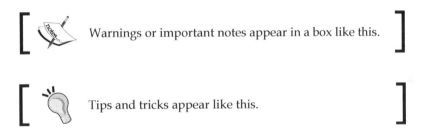

Warnings or important notes appear in a box like this.

Tips and tricks appear like this.

Reader feedback

Feedback from our readers is always welcome. Let us know what you think about this book—what you liked or may have disliked. Reader feedback is important for us to develop titles that you really get the most out of.

To send us general feedback, simply send an e-mail to feedback@packtpub.com, and mention the book title via the subject of your message.

If there is a topic that you have expertise in and you are interested in either writing or contributing to a book, see our author guide on www.packtpub.com/authors.

Customer support

Now that you are the proud owner of a Packt book, we have a number of things to help you to get the most from your purchase.

Downloading the example code

You can download the example code files for all Packt books you have purchased from your account at http://www.PacktPub.com. If you purchased this book elsewhere, you can visit http://www.PacktPub.com/support and register to have the files e-mailed directly to you.

Errata

Although we have taken every care to ensure the accuracy of our content, mistakes do happen. If you find a mistake in one of our books—maybe a mistake in the text or the code—we would be grateful if you would report this to us. By doing so, you can save other readers from frustration and help us improve subsequent versions of this book. If you find any errata, please report them by visiting http://www.packtpub.com/support, selecting your book, clicking on the **errata submission form** link, and entering the details of your errata. Once your errata are verified, your submission will be accepted and the errata will be uploaded on our website, or added to any list of existing errata, under the Errata section of that title. Any existing errata can be viewed by selecting your title from http://www.packtpub.com/support.

Piracy

Piracy of copyright material on the Internet is an ongoing problem across all media. At Packt, we take the protection of our copyright and licenses very seriously. If you come across any illegal copies of our works, in any form, on the Internet, please provide us with the location address or website name immediately so that we can pursue a remedy.

Please contact us at copyright@packtpub.com with a link to the suspected pirated material.

We appreciate your help in protecting our authors, and our ability to bring you valuable content.

Questions

You can contact us at questions@packtpub.com if you are having a problem with any aspect of the book, and we will do our best to address it.

1
Getting Started with Microsoft Dynamics AX 2012 Services

Microsoft Dynamics AX 2012 introduces a lot of new features that are related to the **Application Integration Framework (AIF)** and services in general. Many of the existing concepts have been radically changed. This chapter unveils these new features and enhancements made to services in Microsoft Dynamics AX 2012.

At the end of this chapter, you will have a clear picture of what services are all about in the context of Microsoft Dynamics AX 2012. This should enable you to identify where and when to use services in your solution, and what type of service to use.

The following topics are covered in this chapter:

- **What are services and SOA?**: We will start by defining what services are and what SOA has to offer, and derive from that the scenarios in which they can be used.

- **Architecture overview**: We will look at an overview of the services and AIF architecture, and familiarize ourselves with the key components of the architecture.

- **What's new?**: We will discuss the new features and enhancements that have been made compared to Microsoft Dynamics AX 2009. This is also an opportunity to find out why some of these changes were made.

- **Types of services and comparison**: There are several types of services available to choose from when implementing your solution. Therefore it is important to be able to distinguish between these different types and choose the type that suits your needs best.

What are services and SOA?

So what is a service? The best way of understanding what a service is, is by understanding why you would need a service. Typically, there are a lot of different applications being used in an enterprise. Sometimes this is by design, for example, because a specialized functionality is needed that is not implemented in the ERP system. In other cases legacy systems are not replaced when implementing an ERP system, simply because they do their jobs well. Whatever the reasons, these or others, the result is the same: a growing number of different applications.

One of the problems with these applications is that they are likely to have been built using different technologies. Because they speak a different language, it makes them unable to communicate with each other. This is a problem that services address by providing a means by which applications can communicate, independent of their technology. They achieve this by adhering to standards and protocols so that in essence they start speaking the same language.

A service should have many of the same qualities as modern applications. Applications should be modular, components should be reusable, and everything should be loosely coupled. These principles also apply when developing services. Your services should have a well-defined functionality, and should be able to autonomously execute that functionality without interaction with other services.

Services should also be abstract. By this we mean that other applications should not have to know the inner workings of the provider in order to use the service.

A service is also self-describing, meaning it can provide other applications with metadata about itself. This metadata describes what operations can be used, and what the input and output is. In the case of Microsoft Dynamics AX, this information is published using the **Web Service Description Language** (**WSDL**).

All of these qualities make services usable in a **Service-Oriented Architecture** (**SOA**). In an SOA, services are published and made discoverable. Services are then composed to create loosely coupled applications.

Example implementations

To make the previous explanation about services more concrete, we will take a look at three very different scenarios in which services can be used.

Bing API

Microsoft provides an API for Bing Maps and Search that is available to developers in various ways, including a web service. Developers can use this service for things such as calculating a route between two addresses, locating an address on a map, getting search result for a certain query, and so on.

It's not hard to imagine this service being used in a logistics application, for example, to calculate the most efficient route for delivering goods to customers.

Mobile application

Let's look at a scenario where a mobile application has to be developed for Microsoft Dynamics AX 2012. Even if your mobile application contains business logic to work offline, data will have to be sent back to the **Application Object Server** (**AOS**) at some time. The mobile application could use services to execute business logic and send data to the AOS when a network is available.

A mobile application can also be built without containing business logic, in a way that it only renders a **Graphical User Interface** (**GUI**). In this scenario, the application will have to stay connected to the AOS over the network because the AOS will drive the application and tell it what to do using services.

Business Process Modeling (BPM)

You can use services in an SOA to model business processes. When all requirements for the business processes are available as services, it is possible to compose processes entirely using services. When done right, this is very powerful because of the great flexibility that the combination of BPM and SOA provides.

Architecture overview

Depending on the requirements of your projects, a different architectural approach will be needed. To make the right decisions when designing your solutions, it is important to understand the services and AIF architecture.

Compared to Microsoft Dynamics AX 2009, there have been a lot of improvements made to the service architecture in Microsoft Dynamics AX 2012. The biggest improvement is the native **Windows Communications Foundation (WCF)** support. As a result the proprietary **Microsoft Message Queuing (MSMQ)** and BizTalk adapters that were available in Microsoft Dynamics AX 2009 have been deprecated and replaced by adapters that use WCF. The file system adapter remains intact, and still allows you to import and export messages from and to the file system.

All services are WCF services and are hosted on the AOS. When an application wants to consume these services on the local network, no further deployment is needed, because it can connect directly to the AOS. Just like with Microsoft Dynamics AX 2009, deployment on **Internet Information Services (IIS)** is needed for consumers that are not on the intranet. However, the services themselves are no longer deployed on IIS; instead a WCF routing service on the IIS routes everything to the AOS.

If you want to modify messages before they are received or after they are sent, you can use **pipelines** and **transformations**. Pipelines only apply to the body of a message, and are handled by the **request preprocessor** and **response postprocessor**. You can use transformations to transform a complete message including the header. This allows you to exchange messages in non-XML format.

While not displayed in the diagram, there is now load balancing support for services using Windows Server **Network Load Balancing (NLB)**. Combined with NLB for IIS that was already available, this enables high availability and load balancing for services.

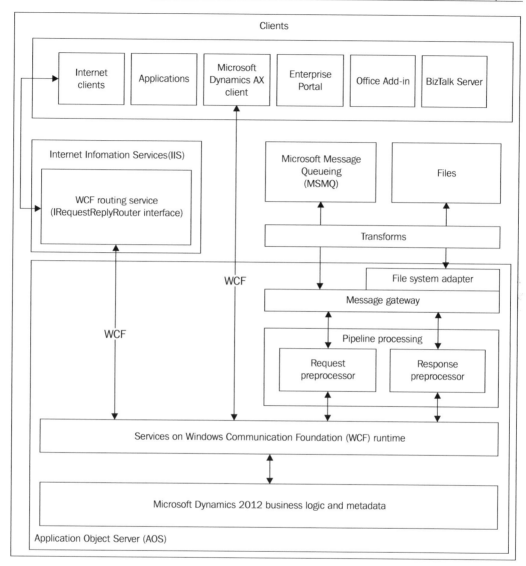

What's new?

Services have been around for some time in Microsoft Dynamics AX. AIF was initially introduced with the release of Microsoft Dynamics AX 4.0 and Microsoft Dynamics AX 2009 continued to build on that. But now with the latest release of Microsoft Dynamics AX 2012, Microsoft has really succeeded in bringing the service functionality to a whole new level. Let us take a walk through the major changes that Microsoft Dynamics AX 2012 brings to the table.

AOS WCF service host

The first major feature that has been added to this release is that the AOS is now the host for the Microsoft Dynamics AX 2012 services. In previous releases, the exchange of messages was either through adapters such as the file system, BizTalk, and MSMQ adapter, or services that were exposed as WCF 3.5 services through IIS. With the latter, IIS was acting as the host for the WCF services.

With this new release of Microsoft Dynamics AX, services will be exposed as WCF 4.0 services hosted directly in the AOS Windows service. As long as intranet users and applications are consuming these services, no IIS is needed.

WCF adapters

Microsoft Dynamics AX 2012 provides a lot more support for WCF. Proprietary adapters such as the BizTalk adapter and the MSMQ adapter that were previously available, are now obsolete and no longer available. Instead, support for MSMQ and BizTalk is provided by a native WCF equivalent of these adapters.

This does not mean that creating custom adapters using the AIF adapter framework is not supported anymore. Custom adapters can still be added by implementing the `AifIntegrationAdapter` interface.

Out-of-the-box, Microsoft Dynamics AX 2012 comes with the following adapters:

- **NetTcp adapter**: The NetTcp adapter is the default adapter used when creating a new integration port. This adapter type corresponds to the WCF `NetTcpBinding`. It provides synchronous message exchanges by using WS-* standards over the **Transmission Control Protocol (TCP)**.

- **File system adapter**: The file system adapter can be used for asynchronous exchange of XML messages stored in file system directories.

- **MSMQ adapter**: The MSMQ adapter is used when support for queuing is needed. Message exchange is asynchronous and uses MSMQ. Note that choosing this adapter type actually uses the WCF `NetMsmq` binding.

- **HTTP adapter**: The HTTP adapter supports synchronous message exchanges over the HTTP and HTTPS protocols. This was already available in Microsoft Dynamics AX 2009, but there is a difference in the deployment to the IIS. The business connector is no longer used for services hosted on the IIS; instead a WCF routing service is used. There is more about routing services later in this chapter.

 More information about the bindings that are used in these adapters can be found on MSDN at `http://msdn.microsoft.com/en-us/library/ms733027.aspx`. If you want to learn more about WS-* standards, check out the *Web Services Specification Index Page* at `http://msdn.microsoft.com/en-us/library/ms951274.aspx`.

Integration ports

In Microsoft Dynamics AX 2009, there was a lot of configuration required to get AIF up and running. This included configuration of the following:

- Endpoints
- Local endpoints
- Channels
- Endpoint users
- Endpoint constraints

Now, integration ports have been added and they provide a simpler way of configuring services. There are two types of integration ports: **inbound** and **outbound**, depending on whether the message originates from outside or inside Microsoft Dynamics AX.

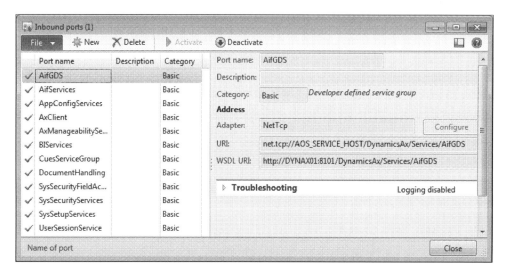

The inbound integration ports can be divided into two types: **basic** or **enhanced**. Out-of-the-box, Microsoft Dynamics AX 2012 already has some services that are associated with basic integration ports. These have been deployed and enabled by default. We will discuss how these basic ports differ from enhanced ports in later chapters.

Instead of having Microsoft Dynamics AX specific endpoints and channels, integration ports use native WCF to deploy services and therefore endpoints, security, behaviors, bindings, and so on. All of this is configured using the WCF Configuration utility. By default, integration ports are hosted on the AOS using the NetTcp binding.

IIS hosting without Business Connector

Previously, when services were deployed on IIS, they used the .NET Business Connector to communicate to the AOS. This has been replaced by a WCF routing service that implements the IRequestReplyRouter interface. Regardless of whether services are consumed from the intranet or the Internet, they are always processed by the AOS. So when services are deployed to be used on the Internet, they will be deployed both on the AOS and on the IIS. The AOS hosts the service using the NetTcp binding and the IIS has a WCF routing service that will forward service requests to the internal services hosted on the AOS.

Non-XML support

Using transformations, Microsoft Dynamics 2012 can transform inbound messages from a variety of formats into the format AIF can understand. Likewise, outbound messages can be transformed from the AIF format into the format required by external systems. There are two types of transformations that can be used: **Extensible Stylesheet Language Transformations (XSLT)** and **.NET assemblies**.

You can create XSLT transformations by using any text editor, but tools such as BizTalk MAPPER, Visual Studio, or Altova MapForce make it very easy. .NET assemblies are DLL files that can be compiled using Visual Studio and do transformations in code. This is especially convenient for transforming from or into a non-XML format. Some of the tools available can actually generate both the XSLT and the managed code needed to compile a .NET assembly.

AIF change tracking

In Microsoft Dynamics AX 2009, document services had a set of six operations available for use:

- `Create`
- `Delete`
- `Find`
- `FindKeys`
- `Read`
- `Update`

In Microsoft Dynamics AX 2012, there are two additional operations available for developers:

- `GetKeys`: The `GetKeys` action can be used in combination with a document filter to only obtain the keys of the documents that were the result of the filter.
- `GetChangedKeys`: The `GetChangedKeys` action does the same as the `GetKeys` operation with the addition of a date and time being passed to the action. This way only the keys of documents that have actually changed since that time are returned.

Custom services

One of the major changes in Microsoft Dynamics AX 2012 is the ease and flexibility by which you can create custom services. Instead of having to provide all the technical details on how the documents need to be serialized by implementing AifSerializable, you can now easily attribute class instance methods. These attributes are used to identify service operations and data contract members.

The SysOperation framework

Prior to Microsoft Dynamics AX 2012, the RunBase framework was used to provide a generic way of creating processes and batch jobs in the system.

In Microsoft Dynamics AX 2012, the SysOperation framework allows you to leverage the power of services to execute your business logic in Microsoft Dynamics AX. When you create a service, it encapsulates the business logic so other components within the system can use the service instead of accessing the business logic themselves.

The SysOperation framework makes use of the **Model-View-Controller (MVC)** pattern by using multiple components that each have their own responsibilities. These components separate the business logic from the code that is responsible for rendering the GUI and the classes that represent the data model. This is a great leap forward from Microsoft Dynamics AX 2009, where everything was written in one class that extended Runbase.

Also important to note is that when a service has been created for the SysOperation framework, it requires little effort to expose the same service to the outside world. You can simply expose it using an integration port.

So the advantages of the SysOperation framework can be summarized as follows:

- It facilitates a service-oriented approach within Microsoft Dynamics AX
- It implements the MVC pattern for more efficient client/server communication and separation of responsibilities
- The GUI is automatically generated based on data contracts
- Less extra effort in exposing business functionality externally using services

Types of services

Microsoft Dynamics AX 2012 already provides a number of services out-of-the-box. These services together with additional services that can be developed can be divided into three types. Each of the service types has its own characteristics and a different approach to create them.

Document services

Document services use documents to represent business objects such as purchase and sales orders, customers, vendors, and so on.

A document service is composed of the following components:

- **Document query**: This is a query that is created in the **Application Object Tree (AOT)** and contains all the tables that are related to the business object that you want to expose. Based on this query, the Document Service Generation Wizard can be used to generate the other artifacts that make up the document service.

- **Table AxBC classes**: An AxBC class is a wrapper for a table and contains business logic that is needed for **Create, Read, Update, Delete (CRUD)** operations.

- **Document class**: The purpose of the document class is to contain business logic that is associated with the creation and modification of the business entity itself. For example, the AxdCustomer class could contain logic to handle party information of a customer.

- **Document service class**: This is the actual service implementation class and extends the AifDocumentService class. This class implements the service operations that are published through the service contract.

When creating document services, developers need to make sure that the business object is mapped correctly to the document query. The document services framework will handle all other things such as the serialization and deserialization of XML, date effectiveness, and so on.

Document services can be deployed using the integration ports and all available adapters can be used.

Custom services

Custom services were already available in Microsoft Dynamics AX 2009, but support for **Extended Data Types (EDTs)** was limited, which resulted in developers having to provide custom serialization and deserialization logic.

Microsoft Dynamics AX 2012 introduces the concept of attributes. **Attributes** provide a way to specify metadata about classes and methods. Two of these attributes are used when creating data contracts: the DataContractAttribute and DataMemberAttribute attributes.

The DataContractAttribute attribute is used to define that a class is a data contract. The DataMemberAttribute attribute is added to methods of data contracts that represent data members that have to be exposed. This way of defining data contracts is very similar to other programming languages such as C#.

Support for more complex data types such as collections and tables has been added so that these types can be serialized and deserialized without developers having to provide the logic themselves.

In a typical custom service you will find the following components:

- **Service contract**: A service contract is an X++ class that contains methods with the SysEntryPointAttribute attribute. This identifies methods that will result in a service operation contract when the service is exposed.
- **Data contracts**: A data contract is an X++ class that is attributed with the DataContractAttribute attribute. It contains parameter methods that will be attributed as data members for each member variable that needs to be part of the data contract.

Custom services can be deployed using the integration ports and any available adapter can be used.

System services

These services are new since the release of Microsoft Dynamics AX 2012. The main difference between these services and the previous two types is that they are not customizable and are not mapped to a query or X++ code. They are not customizable because they are written by Microsoft in managed code. One exception is the user session service, which is written in X++ code but is generally considered as a system service.

There are three system services available for use in Microsoft Dynamics AX 2012: the query service, the metadata service, and the user session service.

Query service

The query service provides the means to run queries of the following three types:

- Static queries defined in the AOT.
- User-defined queries by using the QueryMetaData class in the service.
- Dynamic queries that are written in X++ classes. These classes need to extend the AIFQueryBuilder class.

When queries are called by a service, the AOS authorization ensures that the caller has the correct permissions to retrieve the information. This means that unpermitted fields will be omitted from the query result. Furthermore, when joined data sources are not allowed to be used, the query call will result in an error that can be caught by the calling application.

The resulting rows will be returned as an ADO.NET DataSet object. This can be very useful when you make use of controls in your application that can be bound to a DataSet object.

The query service can be found at the following address:
```
net.tcp://<hostname:port>/DynamicsAX/Services/QueryService
```

Metadata service

This system service can be used to retrieve metadata information about the AOT. Consumers of this service can get information such as which tables, classes, forms, and menu items are available in the system. An example usage of this service could be retrieving information about the AOT and using it in a dashboard application running on the Microsoft .NET Framework. We will create an example dashboard application in *Chapter 7, System Services*.

The metadata service can be found at the following address:
```
net.tcp://<hostname:port>/DynamicsAX/Services/MetaDataService
```

User session service

The third system service is the user session service. With this service you can retrieve information about the caller's user session. This information includes the user's default company, language, preferred calendar, time zone, and currency.

The user session service can be found at the following address:
```
net.tcp://<hostname:port>/DynamicsAX/Services/UserSessionService
```

The right service for the right job

Now that it is clear what types of services Microsoft Dynamics AX 2012 has to offer, the question arises as to when each type of service should be used. There is no simple answer for this due to the fact that every type has its strengths and weaknesses. Let us take a look at two factors that may help you make the right decision.

Complexity

Both document services and custom services can handle any business entity complexity. The document services framework parses the incoming XML and validates it against an **XML Schema Definition (XSD)** document. After validation, the framework calls the appropriate service action. Custom services on the other hand use the .NET XML Serializer and no validation of data is done. This means that any validations of the data in the data contract need to be written in code. Another advantage of document services over custom services is that the AxBC classes already contain a lot of the logic that is needed for CRUD operations.

Flexibility

Document services have service contracts that are tightly coupled with the AOT Query object. This means that when the query changes, the schema also changes. Data policies allow you to control which fields are exposed. When using custom services, this cannot be done by setup, but has to be done by attributing at design time.

Custom services have the flexibility towards the service contract that the document services are lacking. Here the developer is in full control about what is in the contract and what is not. The operations, input parameters, and return types are all the responsibility of the developer.

Another benefit in using custom services is the ability to use shared data contracts as parameters for your operations. Think of a company-wide software solution that involves the use of Microsoft Dynamics AX 2012 together with SharePoint and .NET applications that are all linked through BizTalk. You could opt to share data contracts to make sure that entities are the same for all of the components in the architecture.

In that scenario, you're able to create a data contract in managed code and reference it in Microsoft Dynamics AX 2012. Then you can use that .NET data contract in your service operations as a parameter.

There will probably be more factors that you will take into consideration to choose between the service types. But we can come to the following conclusion about when to use what type of service:

- **Custom services**: Custom services should be used when exposing entities that have a low complexity or data contracts that need to be shared between other applications.

  They are also ideal when custom logic needs to be exposed that may have nothing to do with data structures within Microsoft Dynamics AX.

- **Document services**: Document services should be used when exposing entities that have a high complexity and when validation of the data and structure would require a lot of work for developers to implement on their own.

- **Query service**: The query service should be used when only read operations are needed and there is no need for updates, inserts, or delete actions.

  It can be used when writing .NET Framework applications that leverage the data from Microsoft Dynamics AX returned as an ADO.NET DataSet.

- **Metadata service**: Use the metadata service when metadata information about objects in the AOT is required.

- **User session service**: The user session service should be used when user session-related information is required.

Summary

In this first chapter, we went through the major changes that Microsoft Dynamics AX 2012 brings for services architecturally and saw that a lot has changed because of the WCF support.

Looking at the new features that were added, it is clear that Microsoft has provided us with a lot of new tools and methods for integration. A lot of work has been done to enable developers to expose business logic in a more intuitive way using attributes. The setup is simplified and the system services allow you to build entire applications without the need for development in X++.

There are a lot of options to choose from, so it is not always easy to choose the right approach for your implementation. In this book, you will get to know all of the features to help you do that.

2
Service Architecture and Deployment

There is always more than one solution for a problem. This is certainly true when designing solutions for your integration scenarios with Microsoft Dynamics AX 2012. As we learned in the previous chapter, there are a lot of options to choose from, both for deployment and development of services. In this chapter, we will focus on the options that are available when deploying services.

The following topics are covered in this chapter:

- **What is WCF?**: WCF provides the basis for building, configuring, and deploying services with Microsoft Dynamics AX 2012, so we will discuss the key concepts that are related to WCF.
- **Service deployment**: Deployment of services is enabled by integration ports. You will learn how to create, configure, and deploy these integration ports.
- **Service generation**: There is a lot going on when services are deployed. We will explore the artifacts that are generated, and learn what CIL is.

What is WCF?

Windows Communication Foundation (WCF) was introduced with the release of .NET Framework 3.0. This release of the framework was in essence the 2.0 version together with four additional components:

- Windows Presentation Foundation (UI graphical platform)
- Windows CardSpace (Identity management platform)
- Windows Workflow Foundation (Workflow platform)
- Windows Communication Foundation (Communication platform)

Existing technologies

WCF is meant to provide a unified programming model to build, configure, and deploy services on distributed networks. It combines well known technologies that have been around for some time such as .NET remoting, Web Services Enhancements (WSE), MSMQ, ASMX, and message-oriented programming.

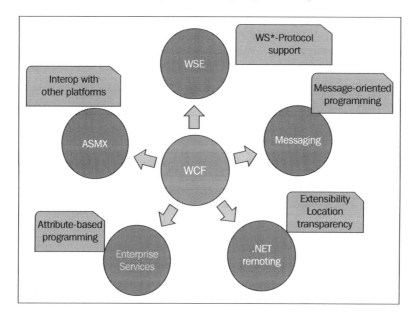

 The previous diagram is kindly provided by `wcftutorial.net`. If our introduction to WCF makes you curious about WCF and its technologies, this website does a great job explaining it in detail.

The ABC of WCF

An elaborate explanation of all the features that WCF has to offer is not in the scope of this book as it would take us way too long. However, one of the important concepts to take a look at is called the ABC of WCF. Each service has endpoints through which communication is possible and an endpoint has the following properties:

- **Address**: The endpoint address can be used to tell consumers *where* the service can be found. It consists of a **Unified Resource Identifier (URI)**.

- **Binding**: The binding actually defines *how* communication is done. It defines the protocol, security, and encoding required for services and clients to be able to communicate with each other.

- **Contract**: Contracts are used to define *what* can be communicated. There are three types of contracts:

    ○ **Service contracts** describe the service functionality that is exposed to external systems.

    ○ **Operation contracts** define the actual operations that will be available on the service.

    ○ **Data contracts** are used to shape the data that will be exchanged by the operations of the service.

The following diagram sums it up. On one side you have the client, on the other a service. This service has one or more endpoints that each consist of an address, a binding, and a contract. After adding a reference to this endpoint on the client side, the client becomes aware of the ABC, and messages can be exchanged.

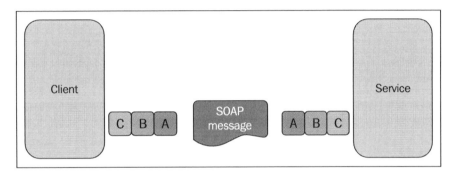

Service deployment

Microsoft Dynamics AX 2012 does a lot to simplify service deployment. Not so much by reducing the number of concepts, but by gradually presenting those concepts to users as they are needed. This is immediately obvious when you look at the setup menu for services and AIF. When you go to **System administration | Setup | Services and Application Integration Framework**, you only see four options. The first two are the most important: **inbound ports** and **outbound ports**. These two types of ports are known as **integration ports**.

Integration ports provide a way to group services and manage them together. They have at least the following properties:

- One or more service operations
- A direction that is inbound or outbound

- A category that is either basic or enhanced
- An adapter
- The address of the port

We will discuss these properties and others in greater detail.

Service operations

An integration port contains one or more service operations. These must be operations from services that all have the same type. You shouldn't mix operations from document services and custom services, because this can cause problems with the WSDL generation.

Inbound versus outbound ports

Integration ports can be thought of as destinations for messages. Services within these ports either receive messages from or send messages to external applications. This gives them a direction. Microsoft Dynamics AX 2012 groups the integration ports based on this direction in inbound ports and outbound ports.

Inbound ports

Inbound ports are identified as integration ports that receive messages that originate from outside Microsoft Dynamics AX. In other words, the destination for the message is Microsoft Dynamics AX 2012. One example of when to use an inbound port (discussed later in this book) is when we create a WCF service and consume it in a .NET application.

Outbound ports

An outbound port is a destination for a message that originates from inside Microsoft Dynamics AX. In other words, it is used when you want to send a message to an external application based on an action in Microsoft Dynamics AX. You can use outbound ports with asynchronous adapters such as the MSMQ and file system adapter.

Basic versus enhanced ports

Integration ports can exist in two categories: **basic ports** and **enhanced ports**. Outbound ports are always enhanced ports. Inbound ports can be either basic or enhanced.

Basic ports

Basic ports can only be created by developers as they are linked to a **service group**. They are created in the **Service Groups** node in the Application Object Tree (AOT). Services are added to the group, and all service operations are exposed when deploying this service group. All basic ports are inbound ports that are hosted on the AOS and use the NetTcp adapter. The WCF configuration editor allows you to change WCF options, but apart from that, there are few options you can set up. Although this makes basic ports somewhat limited in their functionality, it has the advantage that your services are up and running in no time.

There are a number of services that come with Microsoft Dynamics AX 2012 that are deployed by default. You can find these in the **Inbound Ports** form.

Creating a basic port

If you were to press the **New** button in the **Inbound Ports** form, you would not create a basic port but an enhanced port. To create a basic port we will have to open a developer workspace and perform the following steps:

1. Open the AOT.

2. Go to the **Service Groups** node, right-click on it, and click on **New Service Group**.

3. A new service group will have been created. Right-click on it and click on **Properties**.

4. In the properties screen, change the name to SRVTestBasicServiceGroup.

5. In the **Description** property, you can specify a meaningful label. This won't show up anywhere, so this is not mandatory.

6. Next, right-click on the service group, and then click on **New Service Node Reference**.

7. In the properties, click on the **Service** property and select a service you want to deploy from the list.

8. Click on **Save All** in the AOT to save your changes.

9. To deploy the service group, right-click on the service group, and then click on **Deploy Service Group**.

After a few moments you will see an Infolog message letting you know that all service artifacts have been generated, and that your service group was deployed and activated. Your service is now visible in the **Inbound ports** form and is ready to be consumed.

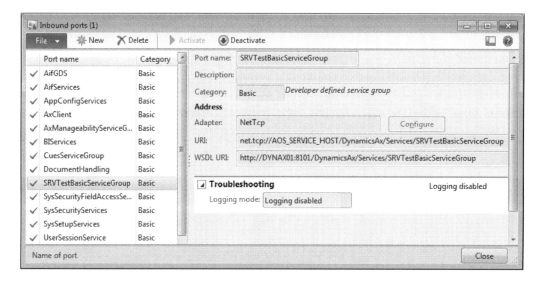

An interesting property on the service group node is the **AutoDeploy** property. Setting this to **Yes** will automatically deploy and activate the port when the AOS is started.

Enhanced ports

As the name suggests, enhanced ports provide more options than basic ports. Unlike basic ports, they are not tied to service groups, but can be created in the inbound ports and outbound ports form. Before we take a look at the options that are available on enhanced ports, let us first create an enhanced port.

Creating an enhanced port

Almost all options that are available on outbound ports are available on inbound ports too. The inbound ports have more options, so for this demonstration we will create an inbound port.

Before we create the port, we first have to be sure that all services are registered within the system. Registering services will insert a record in the `AifService` table for each service, and insert a record in the `AifAction` table for each service operation. These records are then used to populate lookups and lists on the forms when setting up services.

To register services, perform the following steps:

1. Go to **System administration | Setup | Checklists | Initialization checklist**.

2. Expand the **Initialize system** section.

3. Click on **Set up Application Integration Framework** to register services and adapters.

You should register services if you are using AIF for the first time, or if you've added new services or service operations in the AOT. This process will also register all adapters and basic ports.

Now, to create an enhanced inbound port, let's perform the following steps:

1. Go to **System administration | Setup | Services and Application Integration Framework | Inbound ports**.

2. Click on the **New** button or press *Ctrl + N* to create a new enhanced port.

3. In the **Port name** field, enter `SRVTestEnhancedInboundPort`.

4. Enter a description in the **Description** field so you can easily identify the port later.

5. On the **Service contract customizations** Fast Tab, click on **Service operations**. The **Select service operations** form opens.

6. From the **Remaining service operations** list, select the **DocumentHandlingService.create** operation, and click on the arrow pointing to the left to add it to the **Selected service operations** list.

7. Close the form.

8. Click on the **Activate** button to deploy the port.

Your enhanced port is now successfully created and activated. You cannot modify the configuration of activated ports. To modify the configuration, first deactivate the port by clicking on the **Deactivate** button.

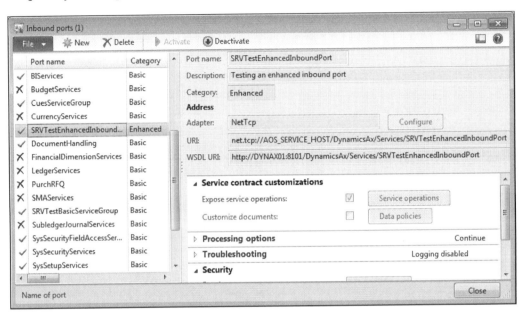

Now that we've created an enhanced port, let's look at the options that are available on the form.

Adapters

Whereas basic ports only support the NetTcp adapter, enhanced ports allow you to specify what adapter you want to use. There are three WCF adapters to choose from: the NetTcp, HTTP, and MSMQ adapters. To exchange messages using file system directories, the file system adapter is available. We will go into more detail about these adapters later in this chapter.

Service operations

With enhanced ports, you can manually select which service operations are exposed. This is unlike basic ports, where all service operations of the services within the service group are exposed.

Data policies

For custom services, the developer defines the parameters that are exposed in the data contract. This is reflected in WSDL when the data contract is used to generate the XSD schema for the type definition. The only way to change this schema is by changing the data contract in code.

When exposing document services, you can change the schema that is generated using data policies. Enabling or disabling fields in the data policies will add or remove fields in the schema, allowing you to manage what fields are exposed or not. It is also possible to mark fields as required.

Transforms

Transforms allow you to transform inbound and outbound messages that are exchanged asynchronously. This transformation applies to the complete message, including the headers. For inbound exchanges, the transforms are applied before the message is stored in the gateway queue. For outbound exchanges, transforms are applied after the message has been fetched from the gateway queue. There are two types of transforms available, XSL and .NET assembly:

- **XSL**: You can use Extensible Stylesheet Language Transformations (XSLT) to transform any XML-based document to an XML document that uses the AIF schema or vice versa.

- **.NET assembly**: When a document is not based on XML, for example a text file with **comma-separated values (CSV)**, you can use a .NET assembly to convert the file into an XML message that complies with the AIF schema. This assembly is a DLL that contains a class that implements the ITransform interface and contains the code that transforms the message.

Pipelines

Pipelines are a lot like transform, but there are a few differences. They allow you to transform the content of the message instead of the full message, and can be used for both synchronous and asynchronous exchanges. They are also run before or after the transforms, depending on the direction. The following table explains the difference between transforms and pipelines:

Property	Transforms	Pipelines
What it processes	The full message including header and body	Only the body of the message
Runs for inbound	Before a message is stored in the gateway queue and before pipelines	After a message is retrieved from the gateway queue and after transforms

Property	Transforms	Pipelines
Runs for outbound	After a message is retrieved from the gateway queue and after pipelines	Before a message is stored in the gateway queue and before transforms
Mode supported	Asynchronous	Synchronous and asynchronous

There are two types of pipelines available:

- **XSL**: This is similar to transforms that use XSL, with the difference that the XSL is only applied to the body of the message.
- **Value substitution**: The value substitution pipeline component allows you to replace one value with another based on a simple lookup table. For example, when messages are sent to a vendor, you can replace your currency code with the currency code of your vendor, such as EUR versus EURO. When the direction is inbound, you can do the opposite substitution. The value substitution is based on Extended Data Types (EDTs). A value substitution map must be created that contains a mapping between the internal and external value for a specific EDT. These maps are set up in the following form:

  System administration | Setup | Services and Application Integration Framework | Value substitution maps

You can easily create your own pipeline components by creating an X++ class that implements the `AifPipelineComponentInterface` interface.

Value mapping

Value mapping is similar to the value substitution pipelines, but it differs in the way that it allows you to substitute values based on business rules. For example, you can replace your item ID with the item number that is used by a vendor.

Document filters

Document filters can be used to filter the keys that are returned when calling the service operations `getKeys` and `getChangedKeys` based on a query you provide. These filters will only be applied when change tracking is activated. There's more about this when we create a document service.

Troubleshooting

On the troubleshooting Fast Tab, you can enable logging for messages. When activated, three options are available:

- **Original document**: When selected, only the original document before it has been modified by pipeline components is stored.

- **All document versions**: When selected, a version of the document is stored every time a document is modified by a pipeline component.

- **Message header only**: Select this option when you only want to store the header of the documents.

To consult the log, click on **System administration | Periodic | Services and Application Integration Framework | History**.

There is also the option to provide more information about exceptions in AIF faults, and the ability to send error messages for asynchronous requests.

Security

On the security Fast Tab, you can limit integration ports to only process requests for specific companies instead of for all companies. Access can also be configured to allow access only for certain users and user groups. For added security, be sure to set these options as strict as possible.

Bindings

When client and service communicate, there are several aspects of the communication:

- **Synchronous/asynchronous**: Messages can be used in a request/reply pattern or they can be used in asynchronous communication depending on whether the client waits for the response or not.

- **Transport protocol**: The protocol used for transporting the messages can vary depending on the needs. Protocols such as HTTP, Transmission Control Protocol (TCP), Microsoft Message Queuing (MSMQ), and Inter-process communication (IPC) can be used.

- **Encoding**: You have the choice on how to encode the messages. You can choose either not to use or use plain text when you want more interoperability. Alternatives are binary encoding to speed up performance or using Message Transport Optimization Mechanism (MTOM) for handling larger payloads.

- **Security**: There are also some options that can be used to handle security and authentication. Security can be done not at all, at the transport level, or at the message level.

As you can imagine, keeping track of all the options can be a little difficult and making the right choice as to how to configure the different settings is not easy. To solve this, WCF introduces bindings. A binding merely is a grouping of choices that deal with each aspect of the communication that we just discussed.

WCF supports several bindings out-of-the-box. If these do not suffice there is always the alternative of creating a custom binding of your own. The following bindings are the most commonly used:

- `NetTcpBinding`: This uses the TCP protocol and is mainly used for cross-machine communication on the intranet. It is WCF optimized and thus requires both the client and server to use WCF.

- `BasicHttpBinding`: This binding is used to expose a service as an ASMX web service so that older clients that comply to the WS-I Basic Profile 1.1 are supported.

- `WsHttpBinding`: This binding is used for communication over the Internet. It uses the HTTP and HTTPS protocols and complies with WS-* standards. So any party that supports the WS-* standards is able to communicate with the service.

- `NetMsmqBinding`: This type of binding will be used when support is needed for MSMQ queues. The `NetMsmqBinding` binding is actually a compact binding which does not provide all the possible options to configure MSMQ. There are other bindings that provide more options.

Now that we have elaborated on some of the out-of-the-box bindings, you might be asking yourself: How can I make sure I'm using the appropriate binding for my scenario? Well, the following flowchart may help you with this choice:

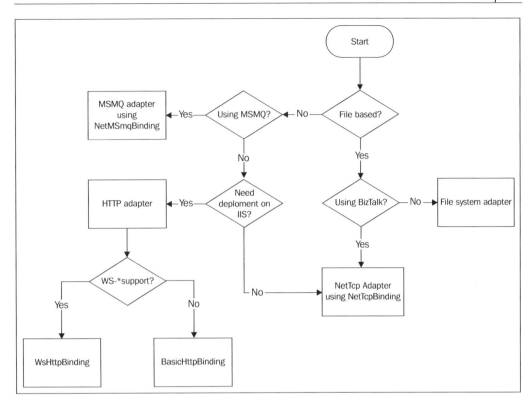

Adapters

Microsoft Dynamics AX 2012 allows for exchange of messages using various transport protocols. This is enabled by the use of adapters. An adapter has an adapter type that determines if it can be used on an inbound port, an outbound port, or both. The standard adapter types that are used are *send and receive* and *receive or send*. The naming of these types is rather confusing, but the following table shows how this translates to inbound or outbound ports:

Adapter name	Adapter type	Inbound	Outbound	Mode
NetTcp	Send and receive	Yes	No	Synchronous
HTTP	Send and receive	Yes	No	Synchronous
File system adapter	Receive or send	Yes	Yes	Asynchronous
MSMQ	Receive or send	Yes	Yes	Asynchronous

Adapters also have an address property. This address is a Uniform Resource Identifier (URI) that refers to the destination or source location of the port. Depending on the adapter, this is a URL, a file system path, or a message queue format name.

NetTcp adapter

The NetTcp adapter is the only adapter that can be used on basic ports. On enhanced ports, the NetTcp adapter is only supported for inbound ports. This adapter type corresponds to the WCF `NetTcpBinding` and provides synchronous message exchanges by using WS-* standards over the TCP.

The NetTcp adapter is used for communication with other WCF applications hosted on the intranet.

HTTP adapter

The HTTP adapter supports synchronous message exchanges over the HTTP. When an integration port that uses this adapter is activated, a WCF routing service is deployed on IIS. This routing service routes all requests to the WCF services that are hosted on the AOS.

The HTTP adapter can be used for synchronous communication when the NetTcp adapter is not an option because of interoperability issues or because the services have to be available on the Internet.

File system adapter

The file system adapter is used for asynchronous exchange of messages using files that are stored on the file system. The exchange is asynchronous because it uses the AIF gateway queue to store both incoming and outgoing messages. A batch job is needed to process this queue. Files are then read from or written to a directory on the file system.

The file system adapter can be used when there is a need to import or export files. The file system adapter has support for non-XML files by using transformations. This adapter can also be used to decrease the load on the system, improving performance. Instead of handling requests synchronously during working hours using the NetTcp or HTTP adapter, messages can be processed asynchronously in batches during the night or in the weekends.

MSMQ adapter

The MSMQ adapter provides support for message queuing using MSMQ. This adapter is actually a WCF adapter that uses `NetMsmqBinding`. Like the file system adapter, this adapter exchanges messages asynchronously and can therefore be used to decrease the load during working hours.

Custom adapters

Having all these features available, it's hard to imagine you would need another adapter. When you do have a scenario that cannot be covered with the standard adapters, consider bringing Microsoft BizTalk Server into the picture. Among many other things, BizTalk can act as an intermediary between Microsoft Dynamics AX 2012 and an external application using any of the adapters that we just described. When this still doesn't fit your needs, you can always create your own adapter. You can do this by implementing the `AIFIntegrationAdapter` interface.

Service generation – under the hood

While services are being deployed when activating integration ports, there is more going on than meets the eye. A service generator written in X++ kicks in and creates the artifacts needed by the AOS to host the WCF services. These artifacts are files containing managed code (C#) and contain the service implementation, message contracts, and a WCF configuration. To explain this, we will take a closer look at one of the out-of-the-box integration ports: the `DocumentHandling` port.

Generated artifacts

When you take a look at the `DocumentHandlingService` service node in the AOT, you will find that this service has one method called `Create`. So when we deploy this service, we expect the following generated artifacts to be able to host the WCF service:

- A service contract which contains the service's interface
- An operation contract for the `Create` service operation
- Request and response message contracts for each operation used in the implementation of the `Create` operation
- A DLL file containing all of the previous artifacts

All of these generated artifacts can be found in the following file system directory:
`%ProgramFiles%\Microsoft Dynamics AX\60\Server\<Server Name>\bin\`
`XppIL\AppShare\ServiceGeneration\<Integration Port Name>`

Service contract and implementation

The service contract definition and implementation can be found in the
`DocumentHandlingService.cs` file. The service contract is a reflection of the
`DocumentHandlingService` class that can be found in the AOT.

```
[ServiceKnownType("GetKnownTypes", typeof(ServiceHelper))]
[ServiceContract(Name = "DocumentHandlingService",
Namespace="http://schemas.microsoft.com/dynamics/2011/01/services"
)]
public interface DocumentHandlingService
{

  [OperationContract(Name="create")]
  [FaultContract(typeof(AifFault))]
  DocumentHandlingServiceCreateResponse Create(
  DocumentHandlingServiceCreateRequest createRequest);

}
```

Let's take a closer look at the code of the service interface:

```
[ServiceContract(Name = "DocumentHandlingService",
Namespace="http://schemas.microsoft.com/dynamics/2011/01/services"
)]
```

The previous line of code defines that the interface followed after this attribute is
the service's contract. The name of the contract and the namespace in the WSDL
are also defined.

```
[OperationContract(Name="create")]
[FaultContract(typeof(AifFault))]
DocumentHandlingServiceCreateResponse Create(
DocumentHandlingServiceCreateRequest createRequest);
```

The previous statement defines that the `Create` method is a service operation
by using the `OperationContract` attribute. It also attributes the type of WCF
`FaultContract` that will be thrown if exceptions occur when this operation is
called. For Microsoft Dynamics AX WCF services, this will always be the `AifFault`
fault contract.

As for the Create operation itself, the Create method has been generated to make use of a DocumentHandlingServiceCreateRequest message contract as the input parameter. The return type of the operation is also a message contract of the type DocumentHandlingServiceCreateResponse. Whether this return contract is actually used in the WCF client depends on whether the service reference is configured to generate message contract types at the client side.

A bit further in the file we find the actual implementation of the DocumentHandlingService service interface:

```
public partial class DocumentHandling : ServiceGroup,
DocumentHandlingService
{
  DocumentHandlingServiceCreateResponse
  DocumentHandlingService.Create
  (DocumentHandlingServiceCreateRequest createRequest)
  {
    // Implementation code omitted
  }
}
```

The previous code shows the class implementing the DocumentHandlingService interface and the actual implementation of the Create method.

Message contracts

WCF uses SOAP messages to communicate. SOAP is a protocol that sends XML messages. It uses an envelope to define what will be put in a message and how to process it. The SOAP envelope contains a header and a body.

In WCF, message contracts are used to provide more control to the developer over the structure of the SOAP message. Although Microsoft Dynamics AX 2012 does not allow developers to create message contracts, they are generated by the service generator. This is important because a call context is included in the message contract that allows clients to pass context information specific to Microsoft Dynamics AX such as the message ID, the calling user, the company, and the language in which messages are displayed.

Message contracts should not be confused with data contracts. While message contracts determine the structure of the SOAP message by providing a mapping between the types and the SOAP message, data contracts are used to serialize the types that are used within the message contract.

The `MessageHeader` attribute is used to specify that a member is part of the SOAP header. In the following example, this is the case for the call context member. For the rest of the members, the `MessageBodyMember` attribute is used to specify that the member will be part of the body of the SOAP message:

```
[MessageContract]
public class DocumentHandlingServiceCreateRequest
{
    [MessageHeader(Name = "CallContext", Namespace =
    "http://schemas.microsoft.com/dynamics/2010/01/datacontracts")]
    public Microsoft.Dynamics.Ax.Services.CallContext context;

    [MessageBodyMember(Order=1)]
    public DocumentFileList _documentFileList;

    [MessageBodyMember(Order=2)]
    public DocuValueType _docuValueType;

    [MessageBodyMember(Order=3)]
    public Boolean _submitToWorkflow;
}
```

WCF configuration storage

WCF services can be configured by using configuration files. The advantage of using configuration files is that they can be configured at deployment time instead of at design time.

The configuration is done in XML by providing elements that configure details such as the bindings, behaviors, and endpoint addresses that are used to communicate with the service. You can also use the configuration file to specify diagnostics elements to enable tracing and logging.

Microsoft Dynamics AX also creates a configuration file to accompany the deployed service. Developers can modify the contents of this configuration file by using the WCF configuration tool, which can be started from the integration port form. The various possibilities of the WCF configuration tool will not be discussed in this book as it would take us too long.

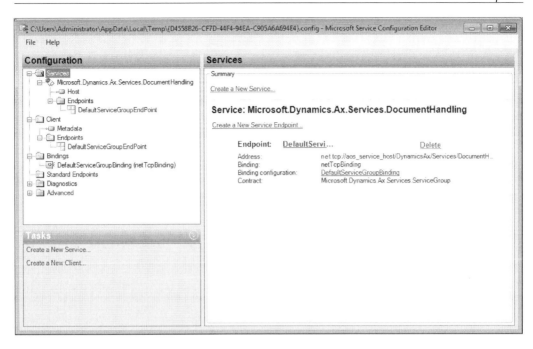

Once the configuration is saved, Microsoft Dynamics AX will save the XML contents of the file in the `AifWcfConfiguration` table in the AOT. When the configure button is used the next time, this content will be opened by the configuration tool.

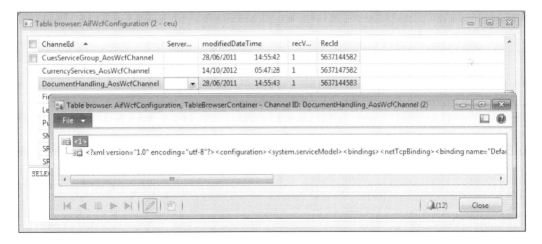

The power of CIL

In Microsoft Dynamics AX 2012, code can be compiled to CIL and run in the .NET CLR. But what does CIL mean and what is it used for?

CIL stands for **Common Intermediate Language** and is in essence an object-oriented assembly language. It complies with the **Common Language Infrastructure (CLI)**, which is a specification that was developed by Microsoft to describe a set of rules which programming languages need to comply with when they are targeting the CLI. One of the most important aspects of the CIL is that it is a platform- and CPU-independent instruction set. This enables the code to be executed on different environments as long as they comply with the CLI specification.

The following diagram shows that the languages are first compiled in CIL, after which the **Common Language Runtime (CLR)** compiles the platform-independent CIL code into machine readable code:

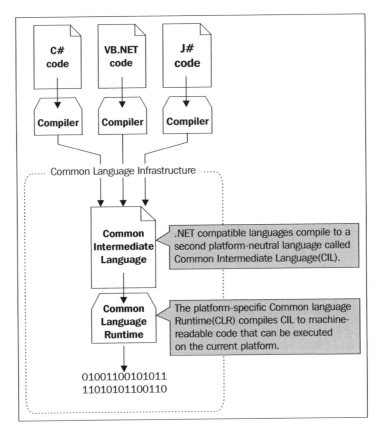

Microsoft Dynamics AX 2012 now has the ability to transform the X++ compiler's P-Code to CIL code and therefore is able to run X++ code in CIL. This is quite a step forward as CIL is faster than X++. We also need to keep CIL in mind when developing services later on. Code that runs on the server, such as batch jobs and services, will be running in CIL and therefore X++ code needs to be compiled into CIL.

As compilation into CIL takes a long time, it is not done automatically when X++ code is compiled. We need to do this manually when code has been modified by using the new CIL compilation buttons in the developer workspace:

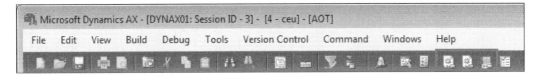

You can either start a full or an incremental CIL generation. The main difference between the two is that the incremental generation only regenerates the objects that were modified since the previous generation, and the full generation completely regenerates all objects. As you can imagine, the incremental process is much faster than the full process, but do keep in mind that incremental generation will not always be enough. Sometimes you will have no option than to completely regenerate CIL. No matter how you look at it, compiling CIL is not optional. Without CIL, your services cannot run!

CIL output

So the CIL generation is done. But what has changed and where can we find the results of the process? The answer to that question can be found in the server's `bin` directory. By default, the file system folder is : `%ProgramFiles%\Microsoft Dynamics AX\60\Server\<Server Name>\bin\XppIL\`. In this folder, you can find the resulting `Dynamics.Ax.Application.dll` assembly file along with a list of NetModule files.

NetModule files differ from .NET assemblies in the fact that they do not contain an assembly manifest. They only contain type metadata and compiled code. Next to these files containing the CIL code, this folder may also contain a subfolder named source. In this folder we can find files with the .xpp extension. These files contain the X++ source code and can be used when debugging CIL code in Visual Studio so that the editor and debugger can show the actual source code.

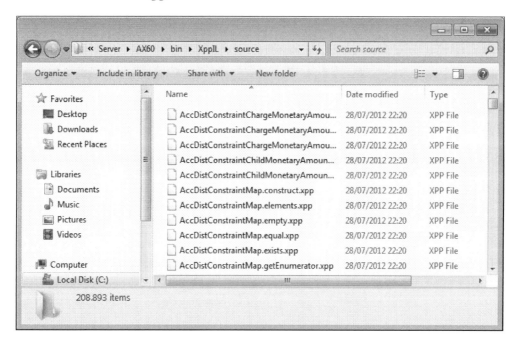

Note that the existence of the source subfolder depends on the server configuration. When the options are set to enable debugging on the server, the source folder will be generated at AOS startup. Without the options enabled you cannot debug, so the source folder will not be generated as this is not needed.

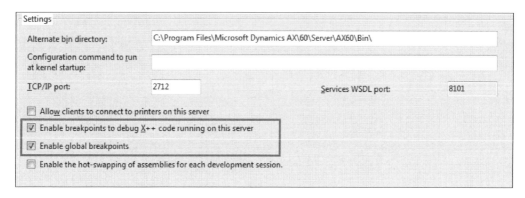

Summary

In this chapter, we familiarized ourselves with the service architecture. We clearly saw that Microsoft has put a lot of effort into providing us with a simplified administration process for services by introducing integration ports. Because a large part of the architecture is built upon WCF, at least a basic understanding of the technologies that are used in WCF is needed.

To enable all these technologies in combination with Microsoft Dynamics AX 2012, compilation into CIL was introduced. This will allow X++ code to be compiled into CIL and benefit from all the advantages the CIL has.

In the next chapter, we will start digging deeper into the AIF services and get some hands-on time by creating our own AIF services.

3
AIF Document Services

When we think of services, we typically think about exposing business logic or consuming it. In many cases though, it's business data that needs to be exchanged. With Microsoft Dynamics AX 2012, the preferred method of exchanging business entities is by using document services.

In this chapter, we will discuss the AIF document services and learn about the components that make up a document service. By the end of this chapter, you will be able to create, deploy, and consume such a service.

The following topics are covered in this chapter:

- **What are document services?**: We start by explaining why you would need document services in Microsoft Dynamics AX 2012.

- **Key components**: There are some components that are specific to document services. It's important to know what these components are and what their role is in the concept of services, so we will discuss their function in detail.

- **Creating a document service**: You will learn how to create a document service and how to configure and deploy the service using an enhanced integration port.

- **Consuming a document service**: After we have deployed a document service, we will consume it using a .NET WCF application, and look at how change tracking can help us in some scenarios.

What are document services?

If you've worked with Microsoft Dynamics AX for a while, you will know that it contains many tables with a lot of data. These tables can be related to each other to form logical entities such as sales orders. Tables not only contain fields, indexes, and relations, but they also contain code that handles initialization, validation, and manipulation of data. When you send data from Microsoft Dynamics AX but especially when you receive data from external systems, you want all of the business logic that is contained in these tables and entities to be executed for data to be consistent. It would be troublesome to have to code all of this yourself when creating a service. Fortunately, AIF solves this by providing a framework and the tools to create these services.

So what are these tools and components? That's exactly what we will discuss next.

Key components

We will start by looking at the framework and its components. The key components of a document service are:

- A **query** that is used in the AIF Document Service Wizard to create the document service

- A **document** class that represents a business entity and contains the business logic for this entity

- One or more **AxBC** classes that encapsulate a table and are used by the document class to create, modify, and delete data in tables

- A **service** class that contains the service operations

Of course, there's more to these components than the few words we've used here to describe them. We will now look at these components one by one, starting with the query.

Document query

Each document service is based on a query defined in the AOT. By using the AIF Document Service Wizard, a document class is generated and XML schema definitions used for XML serialization are derived from the corresponding query. So the XML message will have a correlation to the query object. In the following screenshot, we can see the query for the `InventItemService` document service:

If we look at an actual XML message, we can clearly see that it matches the structure of the query object. The following screenshot shows the XML content after the serialization of the item business object:

Document class

Document classes extend the `AxdBase` class and represent a business document, for example, a sales order. They contain the business logic across all of the tables that correspond with the document. Hence, the details about the underlying tables are hidden from the consumer.

A document class also handles the generation of the XML Schema Definition (XSD). The XSD schema defines the document structure and the business rules to be followed. As well as the generation of the XSD, the document class also contains logic to serialize the table entity classes into XML and deserialize them from XML.

Responsibilities of a document class

The document classes have a number of responsibilities and amongst those, we have:

- Generation of XSD schema.
- Serialize and deserialize classes to and from XML.
- Guarantee the document lifecycle by making sure operations do not violate business rules that correspond with the document.
- Contain business logic that applies to data across tables.
- Providing a means of defining document-level properties. For example, whether a document is an original or a duplicate.
- Handle consolidation of table-level errors and return them as a single list to the calling code.

Let's look at an example document class and analyze it to see how some of these responsibilities are actually handled. In this example, we will take a closer look at the sales order document class: `AxdSalesTable`.

XSD generation

The XSD is generated in the `getSchema` and `getSchemaInternal` methods of the `AxdBase` class. The `AxdBaseGenerationXSD` class is called to generate the XSD based on this document class and its underlying table classes.

```
private AifDocumentSchemaXml getSchemaInternal(boolean
_includeLabels, container _languageIds)
{
  AxdBaseGenerateXSD      genXsd;
  str                     documentClass ;
  AifDocumentSchemaXml    schemaXml;
  ;
```

```
   genXsd = AxdBaseGenerateXSD::construct();
   genXsd.parmIncludeLabels(_includeLabels);
   genXsd.parmLanguageIds(_languageIds);
   documentClass = new SysDictClass(classIdGet(this)).name() ;

   genXsd.setSharedTypesSchema(sharedTypesSchema);
   schemaXml = genXsd.generate(documentClass,this.getName(),
 this.getQuery());
   sharedTypesSchema = genXsd.getSharedTypesSchema();

   return schemaXml;
}
```

XML serialization and deserialization

XML serialization and deserialization is performed in several places depending on the operation being executed. Either the axdBaseRead, axdBaseUpdate, or axdBaseCreate class is used to service the consumer's call. For example, take a look at the axdBaseRead class that is used when performing a read operation. There you can find the serializeDocument method that is used to serialize the document into XML.

```
protected AifDocumentXml
serializeDocument(AifConstraintListCollection
_constraintListCollection, boolean _calledFromRead)
{
  ClassName              documentName;
  Map                    propertyInfoMap;
  ;
  this.init();

  this.setDocumentNameSpace();

  documentName    = axdBase.getName();
  propertyInfoMap = this.getMethodInfoMap(classIdGet(axdBase));

  axdXmlWriter.writeStartDocument(documentName);

  this.serializeClass(propertyInfoMap, axdBase);

  // Omitted code

  axdXmlWriter.writeEndDocument();
  return axdXmlWriter.getXML();
}
```

In the previous code, the following methods are used:

- `getMethodInfoMap` fetches all the fields for the document class
- `writeStartDocument` writes the XML document's begin tag
- `serializeClass` takes care of serializing all of the properties into XML
- `writeEndDocument` writes the XML document's end tag

Cross-table business logic

The `AxdSalesOrder` document class contains logic to handle cross-table dependencies. The `prepareForSave` method is an example of this. This method is called for every record that is saved. Let's take a look at a small piece of the code that is used for the sales document, and see how it handles logic across the `SalesLine` and `InventDim` tables:

```
case classNum(AxInventDim) :
  axInventDim = _axdStack.top();
  axSalesLine = axInventDim.parentAxBC();
  axSalesLine.axInventDim().resetInternalValues();

  if (createRecord)
  {
    axSalesLine.salesLine().unLinkAgreementLine();
  }
  else
  {
//InventDimId marked as touched in update scenarios and we need
new InventDimId
    axSalesLine.clearField(fieldNum(SalesLine,InventDimId),false);
  }

  axInventDim.moveAxInventDim(axSalesLine.axInventDim());
  axSalesLine.setInventDimIdDirtySaved(false);

  return true;
```

In the code, we can see the following:

- In the case of an insert, the link with any possible agreement lines is removed
- In the case of an update, the current `InventDimId` field is blanked out so a new `InventDimId` can be filled in
- Lastly, the values of the `InventDim` table class are copied to the `SalesLine` table class, and the `InventDim` field of the `SalesLine` is marked as dirty to be saved

Validation and business rule enforcement

The document class is also responsible for validating the business document and making sure that the business rules are enforced. An example of this can be found in the checkSalesLine method. This method is called from within the prepareForSave method to ensure that the SalesLine record does not contain any values conflicting with the business rules. The following code snippet shows how two of the business rules are validated:

```
salesLineOrig = _axSalesLine.salesLine().orig();
if (salesLineOrig.LineDeliveryType == LineDeliveryType::DeliveryLine)
{
  if (_axSalesLine.parmSalesQty() != salesLineOrig.SalesQty)
  {
  // It is not allowed to change quantity on delivery schedule
order lines.
      error("@SYS133823");
  }
  if (_axSalesLine.parmSalesUnit() != salesLineOrig.SalesUnit)
  {
  // It is not allowed to change sales unit on delivery schedule
order lines.
      error("@SYS133824");
  }
}
```

The code checks the SalesQty and SalesUnit fields when the LineDeliveryType is DeliveryLine. If these fields do not match, an error is written to the Infolog.

AxBC classes

AxBC classes can be seen as wrapper classes for tables as they provide an object interface to the underlying table. They manage data access from and to the underlying table and contain business logic that is otherwise contained on forms. They also provide a means to specify default values for fields. Another name for AxBC classes is **Ax<Table>** classes.

AxBC classes are optional. It is possible to have a document service in which the underlying tables have no corresponding AxBC classes. If so, the framework will use the AxCommon class to perform read and write operations to the table. In this case you will have to place your code in the Axd<Document> class in the prepareForSave and prepareForSaveExtended methods.

One example that shows how AxBC classes are optional is **value mapping**. Value mapping can be set up in the processing options of an integration port. When this type of value mapping suffices, it is not necessary to create an AxBC class for value mapping purposes. In this case an AxBC class only becomes necessary if you want to do more elaborate value mapping than the standard setup allows you to.

So, depending on what your needs are, you can choose not to create AxBC classes for the tables in your document service. You can do this in the AIF Document Service Wizard. The wizard only creates the AxBC classes if the option **Generate AxBC classes** is selected.

Responsibilities of an AxBC class

The following are the responsibilities of an AxBC class:

- **Performing validation**: AxBC classes make sure that all of the rules and logic contained in the underlying table are adhered to. Things like data integrity and business rules defined on the field level are also maintained.

- **Providing field sequencing**: Using AxBC classes, you can specify the order in which fields are processed. This is particularly useful when the value of one field depends upon the value of another.

- **Performing value mapping**: Values can be mapped between external systems and Microsoft Dynamics AX 2012. Value mapping can be done at the AxBC level if the possibilities provided by value mapping at the integration port are insufficient.

- **Enable value defaulting for fields**: Fields that are not set by the calling code and do not receive a default value in the `initValue` method of the table can be defaulted in the AxBC class.

Validation

In the `AxSalesLine` class, we can see that there is validation logic in the `validateWrite` method:

```
protected void validateWrite()
{
  if (this.validateInput())
  {
    if (!salesLine.validateWrite(true))
    {
      if (continueOnError)
      {
        error("@SYS98197");
      }
```

```
        else
        {
            throw error("@SYS23020");
        }
      }
    }
  }
```

The code shows that the AxSalesLine class also calls the validateWrite method on the underlying table. This is done to make sure that the validation rules on the table are adhered to.

Field sequencing

In almost all AxBC classes, you will find a method called setTableFields. In the AxSalesLine class, this method calls all of the setter methods present for the fields of the SalesLine table.

```
protected void setTableFields()
{
    //<GMX>
    #ISOCountryRegionCodes
    //</GMX>
    super();
    useMapPolicy = false;

    this.setAddressRefTableId();
    [...]
    this.setCustAccount();
    this.setCustGroup();
    [...]
```

When you want to define the order in which the fields are set, you can modify the code and rearrange the setter methods into the sequence that you want. In the previous code, you can see that the CustAccount field is set first and then the CustGroup field. This is because determining the CustGroup field depends on the value of the CustAccount field.

Value mapping

If we look at the `valueMapDependingFields` method, we can see an example of how value mapping can be done:

```
protected void valueMapDependingFields()
{
   ItemId       valueMapedItemId;
   InventDim    valueMapedInventDim;

   if (this.valueMappingInbound())
   {
     if (salesLine.CustAccount && item)
     {
       [valueMapedItemId,valueMapedInventDim] =
this.axSalesItemId(salesLine.CustAccount,item);

       this.parmItemId(valueMapedItemId);

       if (!InventDim::isInventDimEqualProductDim
(EcoResProductDimGroupSetup::newItemId(salesLine.ItemId),
valueMapedInventDim,InventDim::find(InventDim::inventDimIdBlank())))
       {
         axInventDim.productDimensions(valueMapedInventDim);
         this.parmInventDimId
(InventDim::findOrCreate(axInventDim.inventDim()).InventDimId);
       }
     }
   }
}
```

The exact implementation of the previous code is unimportant, but you can clearly see that the `axSalesItemId` method does the value mapping to determine the item number. Then the mapped item number is used on the `SalesLine` record. Apart from the value mapping of the item number, there is also a mapping for the inventory dimensions of the corresponding `InventDim` record.

Default values

AxBC classes can also contain logic that sets default values on fields. An example of this is found in the `setLineNum` method:

```
protected void setLineNum()
{
   if (this.isMethodExecuted(funcName(), fieldNum(SalesLine,
LineNum)))
```

```
{
  return;
}

this.setSalesId();

if (this.isFieldSet(fieldNum(SalesLine, SalesId)))
{
  if (!lineNum)
  {
    lineNum = SalesLine::lastLineNum(this.parmSalesId());
  }
  lineNum += 1;

  this.parmLineNum(lineNum);
}
}
```

In the previous code, we can see the following:

- Firstly, the framework checks if this method has already been executed
- The `setSalesId` method makes sure the sales order number value is set
- If there is no line number yet, the `lastLineNum` method is used to determine the highest line number used at the time
- Lastly, the line number is incremented and set in the `SalesLine` record

Service class

Service classes are classes that contain the operations used in the integration port for that document service. Only the operations needed by the business are available. All service classes extend the `AifDocumentService` class and delegate their operations to the `AifDocumentService` class. For example, when the `Read` operation is available on a service class, the implementation of the operation will call the `ReadList` method on the `AifDocumentService` parent class.

The following operations are available:

- `Create`: This operation receives a document class and creates records as necessary. The return value is an `AifEntityKeyList` object containing a list of key/value pairs that reference a record.
- `Delete`: This operation is used to delete records from the database. The IDs of the records to delete are passed as a parameter.

- `Find`: This operation takes an `AifQueryCriteria` parameter and queries the database. The return value is a document class containing the resulting records.

- `Findkeys`: This operation does the same thing as the find operation but returns an `AifEntityKeyList` object, which contains only the IDs of the resulting records instead of all the data.

- `Read`: This operation takes an `AifEntityKeyList` object as a parameter, reads the records from the database, and returns them in a document. This operation is typically used in combination with the `FindKeys` operation that first returns the values needed as an input for the `Read` operation.

- `Update`: This operation takes an `AifEntityKeyList` object containing the IDs of the records to update. The second parameter is the document containing the updated records.

- `GetKeys`: This operation uses a document filter and returns the resulting document keys in an `AifEntityKeyList` object.

- `GetChangedKeys`: This operation also uses a document filter together with a `DateTime` parameter to return the document keys of the documents that have changed since then.

Service node

For our service operations to be available in the inbound and outbound port forms, a service class alone is not enough. The services framework requires that you create a service node in the AOT for the service and its service operations that you want to expose. This is true for document services, but applies equally to custom services.

A service node allows you to create service contracts based on service classes in a flexible and customizable way. If you wish, you can create multiple service nodes for one service class, each with a different external name and a different set of service operations that are exposed. You can even specify the namespace for the service and change the names of the service operations.

Creating a document service

As you've read, there are a lot of components that have to be created when developing a document service. You might think that creating a document service is a daunting task because of that, but fortunately that is not the case.

Microsoft has provided us with the **AIF Document Service Wizard**. This wizard allows you to create a document service fairly quickly based on a query you provide. In the next few pages, we will walk through all of the steps needed to create a document service using this wizard.

> **Downloading the example code**
>
> You can download the example code files for all Packt books you have purchased from your account at http://www.packtpub.com. If you purchased this book elsewhere, you can visit http://www.packtpub.com/support and register to have the files e-mailed directly to you.

The document service we will build in this chapter will allow us to demonstrate all of the service operations that are available on a document service. We will need an entity from the demo application for this purpose, and for that we will use titles which are stored in the CVRTitle table. At the end of this chapter, we will have built a fully functional document service that can create, read, and modify title information.

Setting the compiler level

Before we start, let's make sure the compiler is set up correctly. When developing for Microsoft Dynamics AX 2012, it is important to adhere to the best practices that Microsoft has defined. These best practices are checked by the compiler. Depending on the compiler level, a smaller or larger set of best practices will be checked during compilation.

We recommend you set the compiler level to **4**, the *maximum*, so all best practice errors are shown when compiling. We also recommend setting the compiler to check the best practices at least on level **Error**. When setting the best practice parameters, also make sure that the layer setting is set to **Check all nodes**.

The layer setting is important when creating document services because it makes sure that AxBC classes that are in lower layers are checked when new fields are added to the corresponding tables. You will receive recommendations about what methods should be created. This is important so that the AxBC classes are up to date.

Creating the query

As every document service is based on a query, we will start by creating the query. Create a new query in the AOT, name it AxdCVRTitle, and add the CVRTitle table to the data sources. When you're done, it will look like the following screenshot:

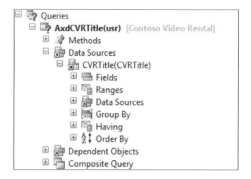

You now have the basis of the query. However, you should see a compiler error saying you should specify the dynamic property on the data source. To set the property, select the **Fields** node of the data source and in the properties form set **Dynamic** to **No**.

Setting the property to **No** allows you to specify the fields on the data sources yourself. You should do this for all document queries. If you had set this property to **Yes**, the number of fields in the document would change when fields are added to the table, and that's not desirable.

For this demonstration, we will add all of the fields from the table to the data source. The easiest way to do this is by setting the **Dynamic** property to **Yes**, saving the query, and then setting it to **No** again.

In a real-life scenario, you should only expose fields that are really needed. If you are unsure, you can still add the field and use data policies to disable it.

To finish up, set the **Update** property to **Yes** on the data source. This will enable us to perform the update operation on the document service using the previously created query.

Running the AIF Document Service Wizard

Now that the query is created, we can use it to run the AIF Document Service Wizard. This wizard will guide you through a series of steps that will generate the necessary artifacts.

There are three ways to start the AIF Document Service Wizard:

1. In the Development Workspace, click on **Tools | Wizards | AIF Document Service Wizard**.

2. The same wizard can also be started by clicking on **Tools | Application Integration Framework | Create document service**.

3. Finally, you can start the wizard by right-clicking on a query, then clicking on **Add-Ins | AIF Document Service Wizard**. This last way takes you immediately to the second screen of the wizard with the parameters filled in depending on the query you selected.

The first screen of the wizard is the **Welcome** screen. It informs you that this wizard will help you generate document services. Click on **Next** and the **Select document parameters** screen is shown.

Selecting document parameters

On the **Select document parameters** screen, you can select the query and specify the document name. Select the **AxdCVRTitle** query from the drop-down list. The **Document name** field is automatically filled in. Accept the name that was generated. In the **Document label** field, enter `Titles`. We will create a label for this text later on in the chapter. Now, click on **Next**:

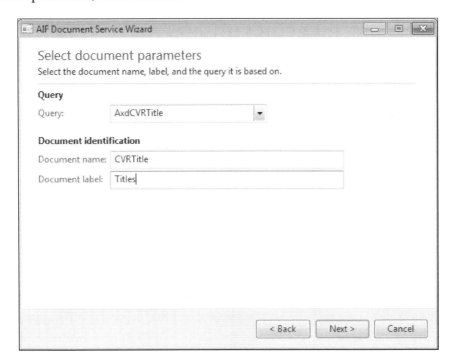

Selecting code generation parameters

On the **Select code generation parameters** screen, you can specify the class names and the service operations that need to be generated. You can also generate AxBC classes for tables if they don't exist yet, or update existing AxBC classes.

In the **Class names** section, you should accept all class names that are proposed by the wizard. The following is how the class names are generated:

- The service class name is the name of the query with the suffix "Service" added and the prefix "Axd" removed
- The document object class name is based on the name of the query without the prefix "Axd"
- The Axd class name is the same as the query name

Sometimes names can conflict with the names of existing objects. In our case the CVRTitle class name will conflict with the CVRTitle table name. So we will have to add "Document" to the document object class name to fix this. In this example, we also add "Document" to the service class name, so we can differentiate between it and another service for titles that we will create in the next chapter.

In the **Service operations** section, you can specify the service operation(s) that you want to generate for the document service. For this demonstration, we will select all of the service operations.

In the **AxBC generation** section, select the **Generate AxBC classes** option. This will ensure that the AxBC classes are generated for the tables we use in the data sources of our query. Do not select **Regenerate existing AxBC classes**, as this may overwrite customizations you've made to existing AxBC classes. Now, click on **Next**:

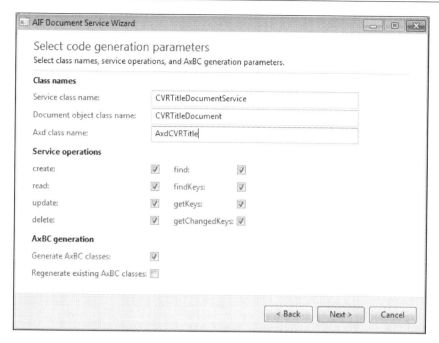

Generating code

You are now presented with a list of artifacts that will be created. Review this list to check for any mistakes you may have made. You can always return to the previous screens using the **Back** button:

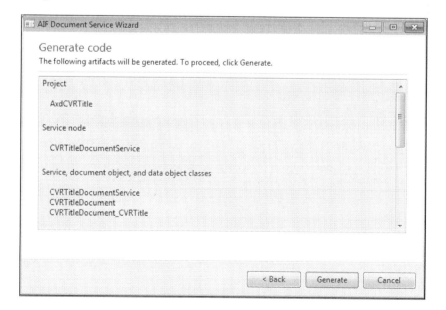

Click on **Generate** to continue. The wizard will generate all of the artifacts and when it is done, a screen titled **Completed** appears informing you which artifacts have been generated. Click on **Finish** to close the form.

Finishing up

The output of the AIF Document Service Wizard is stored in a private project that has the same name as the query that the service is based on. You have to compile this project because it will contain compiler errors that need fixing and tasks that you need to perform.

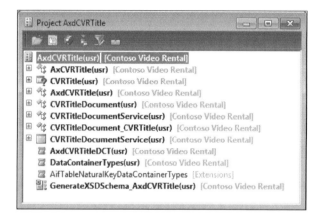

Fixing compiler errors

If you have followed all of the previous steps, you should see two compiler errors for the AxBC class that was generated. This is because two template methods that enable caching are generated for an AxBC class: `cacheObject` and `cacheRecordRecord`.

Caching is used to speed up performance when defaulting values for inbound messages. Without caching, multiple methods would have to construct the same object or select the same record multiple times, thereby decreasing performance.

When you don't want to use object or record caching, you can simply delete these methods to fix the compiler errors. When you delete the methods, remember to remove the declaration of the `cacheRecordIdx` and `cacheObjectIdx` variables from the `classDeclaration` as well. We don't want to use caching in this example, so we will do just that.

When you do want to use object or record caching, you should refactor the methods to fit your needs. The following explanation should enable you to do that.

ClassDeclaration

Object and record caching use map variables that are declared in the AxInternalBase class to store objects or records. As you probably know, a map allows you to associate a key with a value. In our case, the value is either a class or a record. As a map can only contain values of one type, we need two maps, one to cache objects, and one to cache records. This is also the reason why two cache methods are generated, to demonstrate caching for both objects and records.

As each value in the map is associated with a key that allows us to access the value, we need some way to store that key. We do this by declaring an index for each object or record we want to cache. So that's a variable for each cache method we write. By default, cacheRecordIdx and cacheObjectIdx were generated. You should rename them appropriately to the corresponding value. When you cache SalesTable records, name the variable salesTableIdx and when you cache axSalesTable objects, name the variable axSalesTableIdx.

The cacheObject method

You can use the cacheObject method as a guide when you want to cache objects. Unfortunately, the code that is automatically generated is flawed. Instead of using the classCacheInsert method, it uses the the tableCacheInsert method at one point, which is wrong. For that reason, we recommend that you use the AxSalesLine.axSalesTable method to guide you. You can copy the code in this method, replace the variables with your own, and you're all set.

The cacheRecordRecord method

The cacheRecordRecord method can be used as a guide when caching for records is required. It uses the tableCacheInsert method instead of the classCacheInsert method to add records to the cache. The flow is the same as the cacheObject method.

An example of a method that uses caching is the setCustAccount method of the AxSalesLine class. It uses both object and record caching by using the axSalesTable and projTableRecord methods to default the custAccount field.

Fixing tasks

When you are done with the compiler errors, you will still have a lot of tasks left to perform. That's exactly what we will discuss next.

Labels

When you plan on creating a document service, be ready to make some labels. For this small example, over 10 labels have to be created. Fortunately, they are all marked with a TODO in code, which makes it easy to find them in the compiler output window. Create all labels using the label editor and remove the TODOs when you're done.

Generating an XSD job

The AIF Document Service Wizard automatically generates a job that allows you to save the document schema to a file. This schema can be used by external applications so that they know how to generate a valid document. You can change the location of where the XML should be saved in the job.

However, you will most likely change the schema of the document using data policies. In that case, you will have to generate a schema for each integration port on which the document is used. The schema can be generated from the data policies form by clicking on the **View schema** button. This schema will contain only the fields that are enabled instead of all the fields that are generated by the job.

There is no real need to generate the XSD schema when using an adapter that supports WCF.

Constraints

On the document class, the getConstraintList method is generated containing three tasks to perform. This method must be implemented because it is abstract on the parent class, AxdBase. However, constraints are a deprecated feature as there is no way to set up constraints for endpoints anymore. Microsoft Dynamics AX 2012 does offer a similar feature called legal values that you can specify when setting up data policies.

To get rid of the tasks, just remove them and all code in the method that is commented out. This will make sure no constraints are applied to the document.

Validation

Two tasks that deal with validation are added in the prepareForSaveExtended method of the document class. The prepareForSaveExtended method is the perfect location to place the validation for the entity as a whole, so add the validation to it if applicable.

Our example is pretty simple so there is no need to add extra validation. When you do need validation of your entity, a good example is the prepareForSaveExtended method of the AxdSalesOrder class.

Updating the service contract

A very important component that is generated by the AIF Document Service Wizard is the service node. However, you may want to update the namespace of this service. To do this, perform the following steps:

1. Open the AOT by pressing *Ctrl + D*.
2. Go to the **Services** node, and locate the **CVRTitleDocumentService** service.
3. Change the **Namespace** property to `http://schemas.contoso.com/ServiceContracts`.
4. Click on the **Save All** button to save the changes.

Finally, after all of the objects have been created, you might have to register the new service and its operations in one of the following ways:

1. Either go to **System administration | Setup | Checklists | Initialization checklist | Initialize system | Set up Application Integration Framework**. This is what we did in *Chapter 2, Service Architecture and Deployment*, when we created an integration port.
2. Or else you can right-click on the service, then click on **Add-Ins | Register service**, and click on the **Refresh** button.

Fixing best practice errors

The project will contain best practice errors. To check for errors, right-click on the project, then click on **Add-Ins**, and finally click on **Check best practices**. The output will be displayed in the **Compiler output** window.

Privileges

The Application Integration Framework uses the role-based security framework. This means that whoever uses the service operation has to have a role that allows them to invoke that service operation.

You will have to create a privilege for each service operation of the service. To create a privilege for the `update` operation, perform the following steps:

1. Open the AOT by pressing *Crtl + D*.
2. Expand the **Security** node and right-click on the **Privileges** node, then click on **New Privilege**.
3. Rename the privilege using the `<NameOfService><ServiceOperation>` format. For example, `CVRTitleDocumentServiceUpdate`.

4. Right-click on the privilege and click on **Properties**. In the properties, enter a label in the **label** field.

5. Click on the **Save All** button to save the changes.

Repeat these steps for all of the service operations. When all privileges have been created, perform the following steps to add them to the **ServiceOperations** duty:

1. Open the AOT by pressing *Ctrl + D*.

2. Expand the **Security** and **Duties** node and locate the **ServiceOperations** duty.

3. Expand the node, then drag-and-drop all of the new privileges to the **Privileges** node.

4. Click on the **Save All** button to save the changes.

The ServiceOperations duty contains privileges for all of the service operations in the system. This ensures that the system administrators have access to these service operations. When other roles need access to a specific service operation, you should add that privilege to an appropriate duty for that role.

Setting mandatory fields

The Id field of the CVRTtitle table is mandatory, but we want the service to use the number sequence that is defined for the field. The initValue method of the table automatically generates an ID for each record so there is no need to set the field as mandatory in our service.

To achieve this, we will override the initMandatoryFieldsExemptionList method of the AxCVRTitle class so it looks like the following code:

```
protected void initMandatoryFieldsExemptionList()
{
    super();

    // Set the Id field as not mandatory since we are going to use a
number sequence for the Id
    this.setParmMethodAsNotMandatory(methodstr(AxCVRTitle, ParmId));
}
```

If you ever want to set a field as mandatory on your document that isn't mandatory on the table, you can override the initMandatoryFieldsMap method on the document class of your service.

Updating an existing document service

In some cases you will want to update an existing document service. For example, when you have added a data source to an existing document query, or when you want to add a service operation to an existing document service. To assist you with that, you can use the **Update document service** form.

To open this form, open the Development Workspace and click on **Tools | Application Integration Framework | Update document service**:

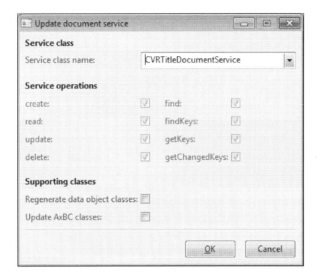

Adding service operations

As you can see in the previous screenshot, you can select new operations to add to the document service. Click on **OK** to add the selected service operations to the document service. This will update the document and service classes so that the new operations are supported.

The only thing left for the developer to do is to manually add the service operation to the service node. To do this, go to the **Services** node in the AOT, expand the node of the service that was updated, then right-click on the **Operations** node and click on **Add operation** to add the new operations.

Updating supporting classes

When fields or data sources have been added to the query of an existing document service, supporting classes will have to be created or regenerated. In this case, select the **Regenerate data object classes** and **Update AxBC classes** options.

When a field has been removed, the `parm` and `set` methods will not automatically be deleted from the AxBC classes so you'll have to do this manually before you update the document service.

As always, after changing the services, it's a good idea to register them again.

Deploying a document service

The development phase of the document service is complete, so now it is ready to be deployed. We need an enhanced integration port for this service because we will demonstrate how to use the `getKeys` and `getChangedKeys` operations. These operations require that document filters are enabled, a feature that is only available on enhanced ports.

The steps that need to be performed to create an enhanced port have already been described in *Chapter 2*, *Service Architecture and Deployment*. Look for the section on *Enhanced ports* and follow the steps in it to create one. Make sure the **Port name** field is set to **CVRDocumentServicesEnhanced** and that all of the service operations of the **CVRTitleDocumentService** service are added to the exposed service operations.

Consuming a document service

Let's head to Visual Studio and start consuming the document service that we created. You can open the Visual Studio project for this chapter, which is included in the code files for the book, to see the service in action.

If you are a more experienced Visual Studio user, you can create a project yourself. In Visual Studio, create a project for a console application by going to **File | New | Project...**. In the **Installed Templates** section, select **Visual C# | Windows**. Choose a project of type **Console Application**, insert a name and location for the project, and click on **OK**.

To add the service reference, in the Solution Explorer right-click on the **Service References** node of your project and click on **Add Service Reference...**. Enter the WSDL location in the address field and click on **Go**. Of course, you'll need to replace `DYNAX01:8101` with the server and port of your installation. You should see a form similar to the following screenshot. Enter `TitleServiceRef` in the **Namespace** field and click on **OK**:

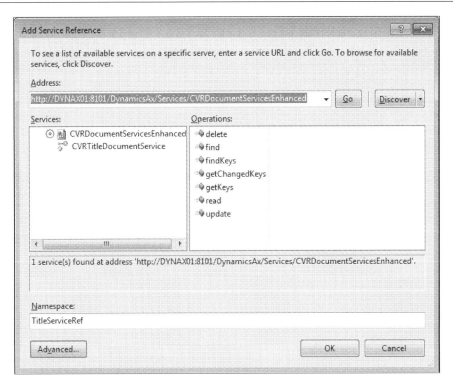

In the following sections, we will go through all of the operations available on the service by using a console application. The console application prompts the user to select the action that needs to be executed. We will only look at the methods that consume the service. For the complete sample application, download and install the sample project for this chapter, which is included in the code files for the book.

Create

The first service operation lets us insert records into Microsoft Dynamics AX. The flow for using the Create operation is as follows:

- Create a new record entity and fill in the field information
- Create a new document instance and put in the table entity array containing the entities you want to insert
- Invoke the Create operation returning the entity keys of the inserted records

The following code reads an XML file containing some sample titles to insert:

```
static void createTitles()
{
   List<MovieTitle> sampleTitles;
   int i = 0;

   // Read the XML file containing the sample data into a list
   using (var reader = new StreamReader
(@"C:\Temp\TitleDemoData.xml"))
   {
     XmlSerializer deserializer = new
XmlSerializer(typeof(List<MovieTitle>));
     sampleTitles = (List<MovieTitle>)
deserializer.Deserialize(reader);
   }

   // For all of the titles, create a title in the Ax database
   foreach (MovieTitle title in sampleTitles)
   {
     i++;

     // Create a title entity
     AxdEntity_CVRTitle titleEntity = new AxdEntity_CVRTitle();

     // Fill in all the fields
     titleEntity.Name = title.Name;
     titleEntity.Description = title.Description;
     titleEntity.LengthInMinutes = Convert.ToInt32(title.Length);

     // For int and real values, you must flag them as fill in
     // This is to tell Dynamics that they are not null, but the
default value
     titleEntity.LengthInMinutesSpecified = true;

     // Create a title document instance
     AxdCVRTitle titleDocument = new AxdCVRTitle();

     // Initialize the list of title entities in the document
     // CVRTitle is a list of title entities
     titleDocument.CVRTitle = new AxdEntity_CVRTitle[1] {
titleEntity };

     // Create an instance of the document service client
```

```
    using (CVRTitleDocumentServiceClient client = new
CVRTitleDocumentServiceClient())
    {
        // Insert the title in Ax
        EntityKey[] entityKeys = client.create(null, titleDocument);

        // Report progress to the user
        Console.WriteLine(String.Format("Title {0} created",
titleEntity.Name));
    }
  }
}
```

After executing the previous code, we can see the titles within Microsoft Dynamics AX:

Find

The Find operation uses a QueryCriteria object containing the criteria to filter on and returns a document containing record entities. The flow for using the Find operation is as follows:

- Create a QueryCriteria object containing criteria elements
- Invoke the Find operation to retrieve a document instance containing the resulting records

Creating query criteria

For some operations, including the Find operation, it is required to pass a QueryCriteria object. Based on this QueryCriteria object, records are queried in Microsoft Dynamics AX. To facilitate the creation of QueryCriteria instances, a method was created, as follows:

```
static QueryCriteria createSingleCriteria(string dataSource
                                        , string fieldName
                                        , Operator op
                                        , string value1
                                        , string value2)
{
    // Prepare a queryCriteria instance
    QueryCriteria criteria = new QueryCriteria();

    // Create a criteria element that represents a query range
    CriteriaElement criteriaElement = new CriteriaElement();

    criteriaElement.DataSourceName = dataSource;
    criteriaElement.FieldName = fieldName;
    criteriaElement.Operator = op;
    criteriaElement.Value1 = value1;
    criteriaElement.Value2 = value2;

    // Put the criteria element in the QueryCriteria instance
    criteria.CriteriaElement = new CriteriaElement[1]
                                        {
                                            criteriaElement
                                        };

    return criteria;
}
```

Using Find

Now that we have a way to create the query criteria needed for the Find operation, we can go ahead and use the Find operation to get the data from Microsoft Dynamics AX.

```
static void getTitles_Find()
{
    // Variable to hold the title document
    AxdCVRTitle titleDocument = new AxdCVRTitle();
```

```
   // Create a criteria element that selects titles that run over
110 minutes
   QueryCriteria criteria = Program.createSingleCriteria("CVRTitle"
, "LengthInMinutes", Operator.Greater, "110", null);

   // Create a client for as long as we need to
   using (CVRTitleDocumentServiceClient client = new
CVRTitleDocumentServiceClient())
   {
     // Find the titles that match the criteria
     titleDocument = client.find(null, criteria);

     // Loop all the titles
     foreach (AxdEntity_CVRTitle title in titleDocument.CVRTitle)
     {
       // Report the results to the console window
       Console.WriteLine(title.Id + ' ' + title.Name + ' ' +
title.LengthInMinutes);
     }
   }
}
```

A part of the result looks as follows:

```
T-000504 Schindler's List 114

T-000505 The Dark Knight 119

T-000506 The Lord of the Rings: The Return of the King 112

T-000509 Fight Club 115
```

Read

The Read operation sounds like the Find operation, but there is a difference. Find uses query criteria as input and returns the title document immediately with all of the resulting rows. Read returns the same document, but does not take query criteria as a parameter. Instead, Read uses a set of Entitykey objects as input. As a result, the Read operation only returns one record for each entity key in the set, because the entity keys correspond to the primary key of the record.

You could be asking yourself why you would want to use Read instead of Find if the latter gives you the same result in one operation. Well the answer is twofold.

The first scenario is one where you have already cached the entity keys in your application. In other words, you already know the unique key of the records you want to retrieve. Then you can just construct an array of entity keys and invoke the Read operation.

The flow for using the Read operation with custom entity keys is as follows:

- Create an array of Entitykey objects containing the keys of records you want to find
- Invoke the Read operation to return a document containing the related records

The following is the code implementation:

```
static void getTitle_ReadWithEntityKey()
{
  // Let the user enter an Id in the console window
  Console.WriteLine("Enter a title Id to look for :");
  string titleId = Console.ReadLine();

  // Create an instance of the keyfield containing the title id to
search for
  KeyField keyField = new KeyField() { Field = "Id", Value =
titleId };

  // Create an entity key instance and put in the key field data
  EntityKey entityKey = new EntityKey();
  entityKey.KeyData   = new KeyField[1] { keyField };

  // Create an array of entity keys and put in the previously
created key
  EntityKey[] entityKeys = new EntityKey[1] { entityKey };

  AxdCVRTitle titleDocument = new AxdCVRTitle();

  // Create a client for as long as we need to
  using
(CVRTitleDocumentServiceClient client = new
CVRTitleDocumentServiceClient())
  {
    // Use the keys to read all of the titles
    titleDocument = client.read(null, entityKeys);
  }

  // Loop all the titles to report to the console window
  foreach (AxdEntity_CVRTitle title in titleDocument.CVRTitle)
  {
    Program.printSingleTitle(title);
  }
}
```

If we execute the previous code for title ID T-000505, the following result is printed to the console window:

```
T-000505 The Dark Knight 119
```

FindKeys

A second scenario in which you can use the Read operation is in combination with the FindKeys operation. This can enhance performance. Let's say that you have a .NET application that queries Microsoft Dynamics AX. It's possible that your query will return a large number of records, but you want to use paging so you don't have to load all of the data at once. So you can use the FindKeys operation to return only the keys of the records instead of all of the fields. Once you have the keys, you can implement paging in your application and call the Read operation with the subset of keys that are actually needed.

The flow for using the Read operation with FindKeys is as follows:

- Create a QueryCriteria instance containing the criteria for finding records
- Invoke the FindKeys operation to retrieve the keys that match the query
- Using the keys, invoke the Read operation to return a document containing the related records

The following is the code implementation:

```
static void getAllTitles_ReadWithFindKeys()
{
  // Variable to hold the title document
  AxdCVRTitle titleDocument = new AxdCVRTitle();

  // Create a criteria element that selects titles that run over
110 minutes
  QueryCriteria criteria = Program.createSingleCriteria("CVRTitle"
, "LengthInMinutes", Operator.Greater, "110", null);

  // Create a client for as long as we need to
  using (CVRTitleDocumentServiceClient client = new
CVRTitleDocumentServiceClient())
  {
    // Call the findKeys operation to fetch all of the keys that
match the query criteria
    EntityKey[] entityKeys = client.findKeys(null, criteria);

    // Check if we had matching titles
```

```
   if (entityKeys.Length > 0)
   {
     // Use the keys to read all of the title records
     titleDocument = client.read(null, entityKeys);
   }
 }

 if (titleDocument != null)
 {
   // Loop all the titles to report to the user
   foreach (AxdEntity_CVRTitle title in titleDocument.CVRTitle)
   {
     Console.WriteLine(title.Id + ' ' + title.Name + ' ' +
title.LengthInMinutes);
   }
 }
}
```

As we are using the same query criteria, we should see the same result as the `Find` operation. A part of the result looks as follows:

```
T-000504 Schindler's List 114

T-000505 The Dark Knight 119

T-000506 The Lord of the Rings: The Return of the King 112

T-000509 Fight Club 115
```

Update

To update records in the Microsoft Dynamics AX database, the Update operation can be used. First you need to use the `Read` operation to get the records that you want to update. For that, you need to specify the entity keys. Once you have the document containing the records that you want to update, you can edit the fields and then call the `Update` operation. The basic flow for updating records is as follows:

- Create an array of `Entitykey` objects
- Invoke the `Read` operation to retrieve the data from Microsoft Dynamics AX
- Update the fields that you want to change
- Change the `action` property on the changed records to `update`
- Invoke the `Update` operation

The following is the code implementation:

```
static void updateTitle()
{
  Console.WriteLine("Enter a title Id to look for :");
  string titleId = Console.ReadLine();

  // Create an instance of the keyfield containing a record id to
search for
  KeyField keyField = new KeyField() { Field = "Id", Value =
titleId };

  // Create an entity key instance and put in the key field data
  EntityKey entityKey = new EntityKey();
  entityKey.KeyData = new KeyField[1] { keyField };

  // Call the findKeys operation to fetch all of the keys that
match the query criteria
  EntityKey[] entityKeys = new EntityKey[1] { entityKey };

  // Create a client for as long as we need to
  using (CVRTitleDocumentServiceClient client = new
CVRTitleDocumentServiceClient())
  {
    // Use the keys to read all of the titles
    AxdCVRTitle titleDocument = client.read(null, entityKeys);

    // Get the CVRTitle record entity
    AxdEntity_CVRTitle title = titleDocument.CVRTitle.First();

    title.Description = "Updated Description";
    title.action = AxdEnum_AxdEntityAction.update;
    title.actionSpecified = true;

    // Invoke the update operation
    client.update(null, entityKeys, titleDocument);
  }
}
```

Delete

As you might have already guessed, the Delete operation will delete records from Microsoft Dynamics AX. The flow for using the Delete operation is as follows:

- Create an array of EntityKey objects
- Invoke the Delete operation to delete the data from Microsoft Dynamics AX

The following code will prompt the user to enter a title ID and then delete that title from Microsoft Dynamics AX:

```
static void deleteTitle()
{
  // Let the user enter an Id in the console window
  Console.WriteLine("Enter a title Id to delete :");
  string titleId = Console.ReadLine();

  // Create an instance of the keyfield containing the title id to
search for
  KeyField keyField = new KeyField() { Field = "Id", Value =
titleId };

  // Create an entity key instance and put in the key field data
  EntityKey entityKey = new EntityKey();
  entityKey.KeyData = new KeyField[1] { keyField };

  // Create an array of entity keys and put in the previously
created key
  EntityKey[] entityKeys = new EntityKey[1] { entityKey };

  using (CVRTitleDocumentServiceClient client = new
CVRTitleDocumentServiceClient())
  {
    client.delete(null, entityKeys);
  }
}
```

GetKeys

The GetKeys operation will return the keys for records that match the document filters configured on the integration port. Each document filter that is configured for the integration port returns a set of keys and these will be combined into the resulting set. Document filters are only available on enhanced integration ports.

Document filter

For the sake of this demonstration, we assume that on the port used by the **CVRTitleDocumentService** service, the following document filter is added:

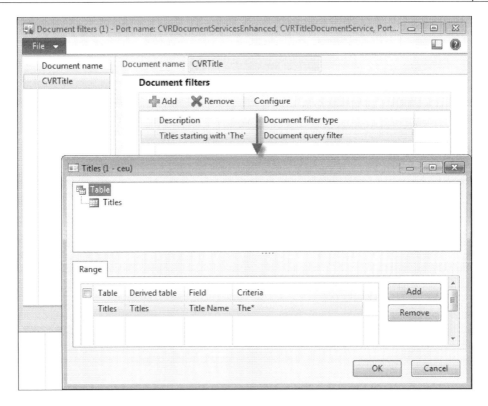

Using GetKeys

The flow for using the GetKeys operation is as follows:

- Create a DocumentPaging object containing the number of keys to return (optional)

- Invoke the getKeys operation that returns the entity keys that match the document filter

- Use the Read operation to retrieve the data of the related records when needed

The following code uses the GetKeys operation to fetch the records from Microsoft Dynamics AX that match the document filter we just discussed:

```
static void getKeys()
{
  AxdCVRTitle titleDocument = new AxdCVRTitle();

  // Create a client for as long as we need to
```

```
   using (CVRTitleDocumentServiceClient client = new
CVRTitleDocumentServiceClient())
    {
    // Call the findKeys operation to fetch all of the keys that
match the document filter
    EntityKeyPage keyPage = client.getKeys(null, null);

    // Fetch the entity key list from the page
    EntityKey[] entityKeys = keyPage.EntityKeyList;

    // Check if we had matching titles
    if (entityKeys.Length >= 0)
    {
      // Use the keys to read all of the titles
      titleDocument = client.read(null, entityKeys);
    }
    }

    // Loop all the titles to report to the console
    foreach (AxdEntity_CVRTitle title in titleDocument.CVRTitle)
    {
      Console.WriteLine(title.Id + ' ' + title.Name + ' ' +
title.LengthInMinutes);
    }
    }
```

Based on the document filter that selects titles starting with "The", a part of the resulting titles looks as follows:

T-000499 The Godfather 102

T-000500 The Godfather: Part II 102

T-000502 The Good, the Bad and the Ugly 97

T-000505 The Dark Knight 119

T-000506 The Lord of the Rings: The Return of the King 112

T-000507 The Dark Knight Rises 103

GetChangedKeys

The GetChangedKeys operation also fetches the keys of records from Microsoft Dynamics AX that match the document filter. But in addition to this, it also restricts the returned keys to records that have changed since a given date and time.

Change tracking

To be able to use getChangedKeys, SQL Server Change Tracking has to be configured. Once change tracking has been configured, the integration ports will need to be reactivated.

Information about change tracking can be found at the following links:

- Configuring AIF for change tracking: `http://msdn.microsoft.com/en-us/library/hh433529.aspx`
- Enabling/disabling change tracking for SQL Server: `http://technet.microsoft.com/en-us/library/bb964713.aspx`
- Enabling/disabling change data capturing: `http://technet.microsoft.com/en-us/library/cc627369`

The flow for using the GetChangedKeys operation is the same as the one for using the getKeys operation. The difference is that you can retrieve only the records that have changed since a given date instead of all records that the document filter applies to.

The following code shows the use of the same document filter, but with change tracking to further narrow the list down to only the records that were changed. This assumes that we have updated records with change tracking enabled.

```
static void getChangedKeys()
{
  AxdCVRTitle titleDocument = new AxdCVRTitle();

  // Create a client as long we only need to
  using (CVRTitleDocumentServiceClient client = new
CVRTitleDocumentServiceClient())
  {
    // Call the getChangedKeys operation to fetch all of the keys
that were changed
    // The change date used here was 2012/07/29 20:30
    EntityKeyPage keyPage = client.getChangedKeys(null, null, new
DateTime(2012, 08, 01, 00, 25, 00));

    // Fetch the entity key list from the page
    EntityKey[] entityKeys = keyPage.EntityKeyList;

    // Check if we had matching titles
    if (keyPage.PageStatus == EntityKeyPageStatus.Success &&
entityKeys.Length > 0)
```

```
            {
                // Use the keys to read all of the titles
                titleDocument = client.read(null, entityKeys);
            }
        }

    // Loop all the titles to report to the console
    foreach (AxdEntity_CVRTitle title in titleDocument.CVRTitle)
    {
        Console.WriteLine(title.Id + ' ' + title.Name + ' ' +
title.LengthInMinutes + ' ' + title.Description);
    }
}
```

As we have updated one record for this sample, the result was:

```
T-000505 The Dark Knight 119 Updated Description for the dark knight
```

Asynchronous communication

So far in this chapter we have focused on synchronous communication using the NetTcp adapter. The file system adapter and the MSMQ adapter work asynchronously and differently to synchronous adapters.

Asynchronous adapters use two tables to store messages:

- `AifGatewayQueue`: The `AifGatewayQueue` table is used in asynchronous processing of both inbound and outbound messages. Inbound messages are stored in this table after they are retrieved by the gateway receive service. Outbound messages are stored in this table after they are processed by the outbound processing service.

- `AifOutboundProcessingQueue`: The `AifOutboundProcessingQueue` table is used by the send service framework to store requests for outbound messages. These requests are then processed by the outbound processing service that stores a message in the `AifGatewayQueue` table.

The following flowchart displays the relationship between the tables and the classes that are used for asynchronous communication:

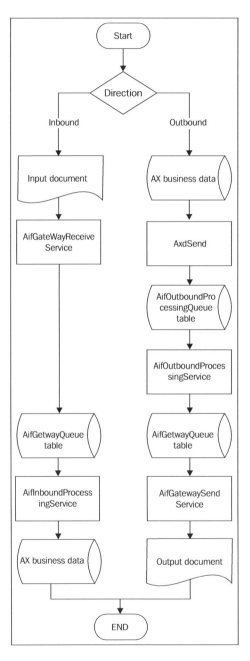

Send service framework

You can use the send service framework when you want to send outbound messages to asynchronous adapters. The following job demonstrates how you can send documents containing titles to an outbound port:

```
static void CVRAxdSendTitles(Args _args)
{
  AxdSend axdSend = new AxdSend();
  AifConstraintList aifConstraintList = new AifConstraintList();
  AifConstraint aifConstraint = new AifConstraint();

  aifConstraint.parmType(AifConstraintType::NoConstraint);
  aifConstraintList.addConstraint(aifConstraint);

  axdSend.sendMultipleDocuments(classNum(CVRTitleDocument),
classNum(CVRTitleDocumentService), AifSendMode::Async,
aifConstraintList);
}
```

When you run the job, the following dialog will appear:

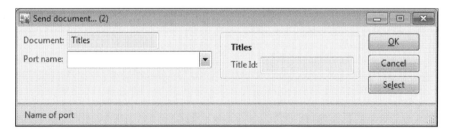

In this dialog you can select an outbound port in the **Port name** field. In order for this to work, you should create an outbound port and add the CVRTitleDocumentService.find operation to the service operations that are exposed by the port. The Find operation is the default operation used by the AxdSend.sendMultipleDocuments method, as this method uses a query. You can change this query by clicking on the **Select** button.

In a real-life scenario, you should create a new class that extends the AxdSend class instead of creating a job. This will allow you to customize the behavior of the AxdSend class.

When you click on **OK**, a record will be inserted in the AifOutboundProcessingQueue table. To process this record we will need to set up batch processing, which is what we will discuss next.

Batch processing

When you use an asynchronous adapter such as the file system adapter or the MSMQ adapter, you will have to schedule batch tasks to process the messages that are exchanged.

To enable batch processing for asynchronous communication, perform the following steps:

1. Go to **System Administration | Inquiries | Batch jobs**.

2. Press *Ctrl + N* to create a new batch job and enter a description, for example AIF asynchronous processing.

3. Select the new batch job and click on **View tasks**.

4. Press *Ctrl + N* and enter AifGateWayReceiveService in the **Class** name field. Also select the appropriate company account and save the record.

5. Repeat the previous step for these classes: AifInboundProcessingService, AifOutboundProcessingService, and AifGatewaySendService. Be sure to add them in that sequence.

6. On all but the first task, add a record in the **Has conditions** grid. The **Task ID** field should point to the task that comes before it and the **Expected status** field should be set to **Ended**. This will make sure the tasks are executed in the correct order.

7. Exit the screen and click on **Recurrence**. Enter a recurrence pattern that fits your scenario and click on **OK**.

8. Finally, click on **Functions | Change status**, and set the status to **Waiting**.

When developing, waiting for a batch to start is not very efficient. The following job processes the asynchronous messages just as the batches do, but saves your time because it can be run manually:

```
static void CVRRunAsycManually(Args _args)
{
  // read the messages
  new AifGateWayReceiveService().run();
  // process inbound messages in queue
  new AifInboundProcessingService().run();
  // process outbound messages in queue
  new AifOutboundProcessingService().run();
  // send messages
  new AifGateWaySendService().run();
  info('done');
}
```

Summary

In this chapter we created our first document service in Microsoft Dynamics AX 2012. Document services distinguish themselves from other types of services because they can be created using a wizard. This wizard creates components that are specific to document services and uses them in AIF.

In doing this, the AIF Document Service Wizard allows developers to create services that are capable of CRUD (Create, Read, Update, Delete) operations on complex documents. The advantage of using document services operations over other solutions such as creating data using SQL statements is that the business logic that is contained in all of the components that make up the service are also executed, such as defaulting and validation of values.

Document services are great for exposing documents, but not so much for exposing pure business logic. In the next chapter, we will discuss a type of service that is ideal for this purpose: custom services.

4
Custom Services

The ability to develop custom services in Microsoft Dynamics AX is not new, but the way it is done in Microsoft Dynamics AX 2012 is. Developers can now create a WCF service in a way similar to how they would develop a WCF service in a language like C#. By using attributes to create data and service contracts, development is simplified as you don't have to worry about the technical details of serialization and deserialization. These things are all handled by WCF, which allows you to create powerful services, fast.

At the end of this chapter, you will have learned how to use attributes to create data and service contracts and how to use them to create custom services. You will also be able to deploy the service and consume it using a WCF application.

The following topics will be covered in this chapter:

- **Key components**: Just as some components are specific to document services, there are also components that are specific to custom services. Most of these components use attributes, so we'll see what that is all about too.

- **Creating custom services**: We will create a custom service step-by-step and deploy it. This service will focus on retrieving data from Microsoft Dynamics AX 2012 and exposing it. In another service, we will focus on a more complex scenario. That scenario exposes business logic that allows you to create data in Microsoft Dynamics AX 2012.

- **Consuming a custom service**: Finally, you will learn how to consume a custom service in a .NET WCF application. This is similar to how a document service is consumed.

Key components

In the previous chapter, we discussed the key components of document services. When developing custom services, there are also a few concepts you should be familiar with, starting with attributes.

Attributes

Attributes are classes that contain data just like normal classes, but the purpose of this data is different. Attributes contain metadata that describes targets. Targets can be of different types such as classes, interfaces, method, events, and so on.

Attributes can either be **intrinsic** or **custom**. Intrinsic attributes are part of the **CLR (Common Language Runtime)** and are contained in the .NET framework. Custom attributes are attributes that you can create yourself.

Because attributes contains metadata, they are only useful when reflection is used. An example of this is a `DataContract` attribute. The service generation process uses reflection on the classes that the service class uses to determine which of these classes are data contracts.

The following code shows the usage of another attribute called the `SysObsoleteAttribute`. It tells the compiler to generate warnings or errors suggesting that the class has become obsolete and should therefore not be used anymore:

```
[SysObsoleteAttribute("You should be using the SysOperation framework
now instead RunBase", false)]
class RunBase
{
}
```

Custom services attributes

When you create custom services, you will certainly encounter some attributes in X++ that provide metadata to the service generation process. The following table shows the most commonly used attributes:

Attribute	Description
SysEntryPointAttribute	This is a mandatory attribute in methods that are exposed as a service operation. It indicates that the method is a service operation. Not using this attribute will result in a service group deployment failure.
	An optional parameter specifies whether the AOSAutorization setting on the tables will be checked when this method is executed on the server.
DataContractAttribute	Defines that the attributed class is used as a data contract for a service.
DataMemberAttribute	Indicates that a parameter method is a data member in a data contract for a service.
AifCollectionTypeAttribute	This attributes specifies the type that is used in a collection. It contains the name of the parameter that is targeted and the types of the objects that are contained in the collection.

Data contracts

Because a service and client don't necessarily use the same types internally, they must agree on the type they will use to exchange data. This agreement, or contract if you will, is called a **data contract**, and is used to describe these data types. The data contract is then used to serialize and deserialize the type.

Services use data contracts to describe the parameters and the return types for their service operations. However, there are some types that can be serialized without using data contracts. The following types serve as implicit data contracts:

- Primitive types (such as str, int, int64, real, guid, utcdatetime, and date)
- Extended data types
- Base enums
- Collections in which all elements are the same type and are of a type that is a valid data contract
- Tables and views

One noticeable exception is the X++ AnyType type, which cannot be used in data contracts. On the other hand, any .NET type that can be serialized by WCF can be used as a data contract, which more than makes up for that.

If you need types other than the ones that are described in the preceding table, you can always create your own data contract in X++. A data contract can be created in the AOT by creating a new class, and by adding the `DataContractAttribute` attribute to the class declaration. You will do this a lot when developing custom services.

Of course, a class without properties cannot hold any data, so to complete the data contract you must add data members in the form of methods. You can use the `DataMemberAttribute` attribute to specify that a method is a data member. The data members themselves can use data contracts or any of the types described previously as return types and parameters.

Service contracts

When we talked about the WCF, we saw that a service contract describes the functionality that is exposed. In Microsoft Dynamics AX 2012, you can create a service contract by creating a class in the AOT. This class is called a **service class**. A service class does not need an attribute to specify that it is a service contract, although it is required that this class has the **RunOn** property set to **Server**.

But when you create such a class, all you have is just a regular class that runs on the server when it is executed. What makes a class a true service class is having methods that are service operations. These methods must have the `SysEntryPointAttribute` attribute to indicate that they are service operations.

Collection types

X++ does not know strongly-typed collections, so when we want to return or receive a collection of data contracts, we have to use `AifCollectionTypeAttribute`. This attribute is used to specify the type of the collection, both for parameters and return types.

It's possible to specify the following five parameters when using the attribute:

Parameter	Description
Parameter name	Specifies for which parameter the attribute applies. This is either the name of the parameter, or `return` for return values.
Item type	The base type of the collection, or key value when the collection is a map.
Extended type name	When the type is `Class`, `Enum`, or `UserType`, this specifies the name of the type.

Parameter	Description
Value type	When the collection type is a map, this is the type of the value in the map.
Value extended type name	When the collection type is a map, and the type is Class, Enum, or UserType, this specifies the name of the type.

Creating custom services

In this section, we will discuss two custom services. One service focuses on exposing data from Microsoft Dynamics AX 2012, the other on exposing business logic.

The Title service

We will use the CVRTitleService service as an example to demonstrate how to create a simple yet powerful service. The service will allow an external program to do the following two things:

- Retrieve details of a title based on its ID
- Retrieve a list of all titles

The Title data contract

Let's start by creating a new class for the data contract that will contain the data for one title. Create a new class and name it CVRTitleContract. In the class declaration, add DataContractAttribute to specify that the class is a data contract. Also declare the variable's ID, name, and description as shown in the following code snippet:

```
[DataContractAttribute('Title')]
public class CVRTitleDataContract
{
  CVRTitleId     id;
  CVRTitleName   name;
  Description    description;
}
```

Next, add three parameter methods, one for each of the properties of the data contract. Use DataMemberAttribute to indicate that the methods are data contract members:

```
[DataMemberAttribute('Description')]
public Description parmDescription(Description _description =
description)
{
```

```
    ;
    description = _description;
    return description;
}


[DataMemberAttribute('Id')]
public CVRTitleId parmId(CVRTitleId _id = id)
{
    ;
    id = _id;
    return id;
}


[DataMemberAttribute('Name')]
public CVRTitleName parmName(CVRTitleName _name = name)
{
    ;
    name = _name;
    return name;
}
```

As you can see in the preceding code, we construct the attributes using an optional string parameter. This parameter is the name. Because we do that, a client application can get the value of a member using code such as title.Description. If we didn't pass a name, the client application would have to use CVRTitleDataContract. parmDescription instead, which doesn't look as neat. It's better not to expose the prefixes and other naming conventions specific to Microsoft Dynamics AX such as the DataContract suffix and parm prefix.

Essentially, you now have a functional data contract. However, there are a few tweaks that we can still perform when constructing the data contract. Because our contract is tied to a record of the type CVRTitle, we can create a static new method that creates an instance of the data contract based on a record of this type. Note, these steps are optional, but performing them has the following main advantages:

- In Microsoft Dynamics AX 2012, it is impossible to create an instance of the contract in a way other than that the developer intended, because both the new and construct method are not publicly available. This way a developer is less likely to make mistakes.

- When creating an instance of the data contract, you will have less coding to do because the contract is filled in the static new method. This will make your code cleaner and easier to understand.

Start by overriding the `new` method, and set it as `protected` so only the `CVRTitleDataContract` class or one of its subclasses can call the method:

```
protected void new()
{
}
```

Always create a `construct` method for your classes, but if it doesn't return a valid instance, set it as `private`. A valid instance means that when constructed, all of the variables needed for execution have to be initialized. Creating an instance of the data contract using the `construct` method isn't valid in this case because the properties `id`, `name`, and `description` are not set.

```
private static CVRTitleDataContract construct()
{
    return new CVRTitleDataContract();
}
```

Finally, create a static `new` method that takes a `CVRTitle` record as a parameter, uses it to construct an instance of the `CVRTitleDataContract` class, and returns it:

```
public static CVRTitleDataContract newFromTableRecord(CVRTitle _
title)
{
    CVRTitleDataContract contract = CVRTitleDataContract::construct();
    ;

    contract.parmId(_title.Id);
    contract.parmName(_title.Name);
    contract.parmDescription(_title.Description);

    return contract;
}
```

Best practices

These recommendations are based on the best practices defined by Microsoft at `http://msdn.microsoft.com/en-us/library/aa854210.aspx`.

So there you go, you have created your first data contract. That wasn't too hard, was it? Now let's see how we can create a list data contract, which is a little more complex.

The Title list data contract

We will create a list data contract using the data contract that we just created. Start by creating a new class, and name it CVRTitleListDataContract. Add the DataContractAttribute attribute to it to declare that the class is a data contract, and add a list variable that will store a list of titles:

```
[DataContractAttribute]
public class CVRTitleListDataContract
{
    List    titleList;
}
```

Next, we add the usual constructers, new and construct. Also, don't forget to initialize the list object:

```
protected void new()
{
    titleList = new List(Types::Class);
}

public static CVRTitleListDataContract construct()
{
    return new CVRTitleListDataContract();
}
```

Next, we have to provide a way to add titles to the list. Add a method that takes a title data contract and adds it to the end of the list, as shown in the following code snippet:

```
public void addTitleToList(CVRTitleDataContract _titleDataContract)
{
    titleList.addEnd(_titleDataContract);
}
```

Finally, we add the data member method that will return a list of titles. Add the DataMemberAttribute attribute as you would for every other data member, but also add two more attributes of the type AifCollectionTypeAttribute, as shown here:

```
[DataMemberAttribute
,AifCollectionTypeAttribute('return', Types::Class,
classstr(CVRTitleDataContract))
,AifCollectionTypeAttribute('_titleList', Types::Class, classstr(CVRTi
tleDataContract))]
public List parmTitleList(List _titleList = titleList)
```

```
  {
    titleList = _titleList;
    return titleList;
  }
```

As we've discussed before, the `AifCollectionTypeAttribute` attribute is used to specify the type of the list, because X++ does not support strongly-typed lists. In this case, `AifCollectionTypeAttribute` takes the following three parameters:

- The name of the parameter, in this example `_titleList`. For the return value, the name is `return`.
- The base type of the type, which is `Class` in this example.
- The name of the type, in our case the class name is `CVRTitleDataContract`.

This concludes the creation of the two contracts that we will need for our service. Now let's see how we can use them.

The Title service class

We will create a service class that has the following two service operations:

- An operation that returns the details of a title based on its ID
- An operation that returns all of the titles

First, we create a service class. Create a new class and name it `CVRTitleService`. We do not need to add anything more to the class declaration, because a service class declaration does not need an attribute.

```
public class CVRTitleService
{
}
```

One thing we have to make sure is that this class runs on the server when it is executed. To do this, right-click on the class, then click **Properties**, and set the **RunOn** property to **Server**.

The Title list service operation

Ok, let's create a service operation that retrieves the details of a title based on its ID. Start by creating a new method. You can see the source code of this method in the following snippet. As you can see, we add the `SysEntryPointAttribute` attribute to specify that the method is a service operation. We add `true` between brackets when constructing the attribute to specify that AOS authorization has to be performed when the code runs on the server. This will make sure that the user that calls the service operations has the necessary permissions on the tables that the method uses.

```
[SysEntryPointAttribute(true)]
public CVRTitleDataContract getTitle(CVRTitleId _titleId)
{
    CVRTitleDataContract    contract;
    ;

    contract = CVRTitleDataContract::newFromTableRecord
(CVRTitle::find(_titleId));

    return contract;
}
```

As you can see further in the method, we use the `_titleId` parameter to find the record in the database, and construct a new data contract with it. Then we return the data contract.

The Title list service operation

This service operation will use the list data contract to return a list of all titles. As you can see in the following code, all titles in the `CVRTitle` table are traversed. Then a data contract is constructed, and is added to the list contract. Finally, a list contract containing the details of all of the titles is returned:

```
[SysEntryPointAttribute(true)]
public CVRTitleListDataContract getAllTitles()
{
    CVRTitleListDataContract titleListDataContract =
CVRTitleListDataContract::construct();
    CVRTitleDataContract    titleContract;
    CVRTitle                titleRecord;
    ;

    while select titleRecord
    {
```

```
    // Convert the record to a data contract
    titleContract = CVRTitleDataContract::newFromTableRecord
(titleRecord);

    // Add the title data contract to the list of data contracts
    titleListDataContract.addTitleToList(titleContract);
  }

  return titleListDataContract;
}
```

The Title service contract

The final thing we have to do before we can deploy our service, is define the service contract. To create the service contract, follow these steps:

1. Open the AOT by pressing *Crtl + D*.
2. Right-click on the **Services** node, and then click **New Service**.
3. Right-click on the newly created service, and then click **Properties**.
4. Change the **Name** and **Class** properties to **CVRTitleService**.
5. Change the **Namespace** property to **http://schemas.contoso.com/ServiceContracts**.
6. Expand the **CVRTitleService** node, right-click on **Operations**, and click **Add Operation**.
7. The **Add service operations** form pops up. Select the **Add** field for the **getAllTitles** and **getTitle** methods, then Click **OK**.
8. Click on the **Save All** button to save the changes.

Deploy the service

To deploy our custom services, we will use a basic port. For this reason, we need to add the services that we want to deploy to a service group. We will add all of them to one service group: **CVRCustomServices**. Let us deploy our custom service by following these steps:

1. Open the AOT by pressing *Crtl + D*.
2. Right-click on the **Service Groups** node, and then click **New Service Group**.
3. Right-click on the newly created service group, and then select **Properties**.
4. Change the value of the **Name** property to **CVRCustomServices**.
5. Right-click on the service group and select **New Service Node Reference**.

6. Select the service node reference that was added and change the **Service** property to **CVRTitleService**.

7. And finally, right-click the service group and click **Deploy Service Group** to deploy the service.

Now that you have completed these steps, go to **System administration | Setup | Services and Application Integration Framework | Inbound ports**. The **CVRCustomServices** inbound port is available there as a basic inbound port, and is now ready to be consumed.

The rental service

The contracts and service operations that we have made for retrieving titles are pretty simple. That might be all you need in a real life application. However, it is more likely that you will need data contracts that are more complex. To demonstrate this, we've added the rental service to the demo application. The rental service allows external applications to retrieve rental information, or create rentals.

Creating this service with all data contracts step-by-step would take too long, so we will only discuss the artifacts at a high level, starting with the database schema of the tables that we will use.

Rental header and line tables

The following is a simple schema of the tables that we will use. A rental header contains information about the rental such as the store and the transaction date. A rental header is related to one or more lines that contain the details of the rental, such as the item that was rented.

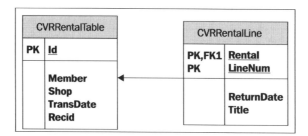

Rental service operations

There are three service operations available in the rental service:

- `CreateRental`: This service operation takes a parameter of type `CVRRentalDocumentDataContract` and uses it to register a rental in the `CVRRentalTable` and `CVRRental` line tables

- `GetAllRentals`: Returns a list of `CVRRentalDocumentDataContract` data contracts by using the `CVRRentalDocumentListDataContract` data contract

- `GetAllRentalsForMember`: This service operation does the same as the `GetAllRentals` operation, but only returns rentals for a specific member

Rental data contracts

There are a total of five data contracts that the rental service uses. The relationships between these data contracts and the service operations are explained in the following diagram:

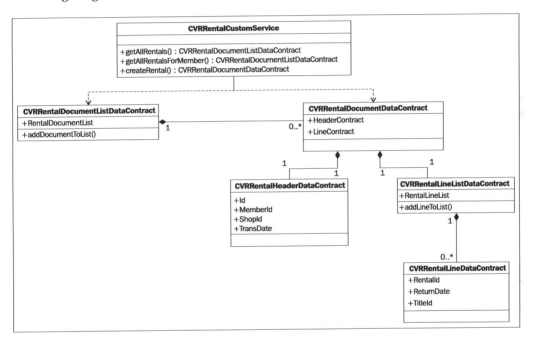

From the bottom up, these are the contracts and their function:

- `CVRRentalLineDataContract`: This data contract contains the properties of a rental line, including the title and the return date.

- `CVRRentalLineListDataContract`: This data contract contains a list of lines. It uses `AifCollectionTypeAttribute` to describe that the list contains items of the `CVRRentalLineDataContract` type.

- `CVRRentalHeaderDataContract`: This data contract contains the header information about a rental, including the member ID and the transaction date.

- `CVRRentalDocumentDataContract`: This data contract represents a rental document. It contains a header and a list of lines, respectively using the `CVRRentalHeaderDataContract` and `CVRRentalLineListDataContract` types.

- `CVRRentalDocumentListDataContract`: This data contract contains a list of rental documents and is used in the `getAllRentals` and `getAllRentalsForMember` service operations.

This demonstrates that you can use data contracts within data contracts to make logical entities. Although at first glance it might seem complex, each class has its own responsibilities, which makes them re-usable and easier to maintain.

The createRental service operation

Following is the `createRental` service operation. It uses the rental document data contract to register a rental in the database:

```
[SysEntryPointAttribute(true)]
public CVRRentalRefRecId createRental(CVRRentalDocumentDataContract
_rentalDocument)
{
  CVRRentalTable rentalTable;
  CVRRentalLine   rentalLine;

  CVRRentalLineDataContract       lineDataContract;
  CVRRentalLineListDataContract  lineListDataContract;

  ListEnumerator   enumerator;
  ;

  // Insert the rental header
  rentalTable.clear();
  rentalTable.Id = _rentalDocument.parmHeaderContract().parmId();
  rentalTable.Member = CVRMember::find(_rentalDocument.
parmHeaderContract().parmMemberId()).RecId;
  rentalTable.Shop = CVRShop::find(_rentalDocument.
parmHeaderContract().parmShopId()).RecId;
  rentalTable.TransDate  = _rentalDocument.parmHeaderContract().
parmTransDate();
  rentalTable.insert();

  // Get the list of rental lines
```

```
lineListDataContract = _rentalDocument.parmLinesContract();

// Initialize an enumerator to loop the lines
enumerator = lineListDataContract.parmRentalLineList().
getEnumerator();

// As long as we have lines
while(enumerator.moveNext())
{
  // Get the current line
  lineDataContract = enumerator.current();

  rentalLine.clear();
  rentalLine.Rental = rentalTable.RecId;
  rentalLine.Title = CVRTitle::find(lineDataContract.parmTitleId()).
RecId;
  rentalLine.ReturnDate = lineDataContract.parmReturnDate();
  rentalLine.insert();
}

return rentalTable.RecId;
}
```

Now, let's see how we can consume the services that we have made using a .NET WCF application.

Consuming the service

Now that we have created and exposed our custom services, they are ready to be consumed. To do this, we use Visual Studio and write two code samples.

Example 1 – Retrieving titles

This first example of consuming the service deals with the retrieval of a title list. We want to be able to write a list of titles to the console window.

Adding the service reference

To add the service reference, perform the following steps:

1. In Visual Studio, create a console application.
2. Right-click on the **Service References** node and select the **Add Service Reference...** button. The **Add Service Reference** window opens.

3. In the **Address** drop-down box, specify **http://DYNAX01:8101/DynamicsAx/Services/CVRCustomServices** as the address for the service and then press **Go**. The address is queried and the services and operations that are available are listed.

4. In the **Namespace** dialog box, specify the namespace that you want to use: **AxCustomServicesRef**.

After performing these steps, the **Add Service Reference** window should look similar to the one shown in the following screenshot. On the left-hand side of the window, the services that were found are listed. In our case, we see **CVRCustomServices** along with the three other services that are contained in the service group. On the right-hand side of the window, we see the operations that are available for the selected service:

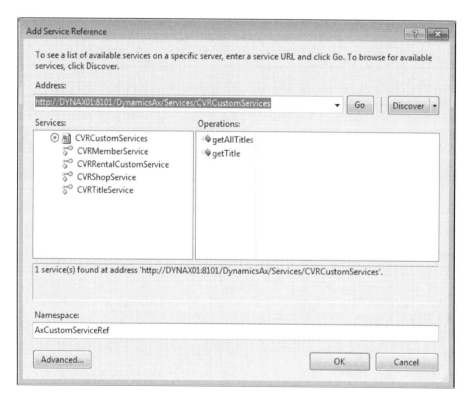

When you press **OK,** the ServiceModel Metadata Utility (SvcUtil.exe) creates a client proxy and types according to the metadata found in the service WSDL. You can view the types by opening the **Object Browser** menu.

Consuming the service

To consume the service and retrieve a list of titles, you can use the following code:

```
static void Main(string[] args)
{
  // Create an instance of the proxy client
  CVRTitleServiceClient theClient = new CVRTitleServiceClient();

  // Create the call context
  CallContext theContext = new CallContext();
  theContext.Company = "CEU";
  theContext.Language = "EN-US";
  theContext.LogonAsUser = "UserName";

  // Invoke the getAllTitles service operation
  CVRTitleListDataContract theListContract = theClient.
getAllTitles(theContext);

  // Loop all of the returned titles
  foreach (Title title in theListContract.parmTitleList)
  {
    Console.WriteLine(String.Format("{0} - {1} - {2}", title.Id,
title.Name, title.Description));
  }

  // Wait for the user to press a key
  Console.Read();
}
```

The output should be a title list as seen here:

```
Title 001 - Memento - Memento weird movie
Title 002 - Lord of the rings - Lord of the rings long movie
```

Example 2 – Register a rental

In this second example, we will consume a service that enables us to register a rental. We will again take a look at creating the service reference but focus a little more on some advanced options available to us when creating the service reference.

Creating the service reference – Advanced

We added a service reference in the previous sample, so first delete it. This allows us to recreate the service reference for this sample and look at it in more detail.

To create the service reference again, follow these steps:

1. In the **Solution Explorer** panel, right-click on the **Service References** node and click **Add Service Reference....** The **Add Service Reference** window opens.

2. In the **Address** drop-down box, specify **http://DYNAX01:8101/DynamicsAx/ Services/CVRCustomServices** as the address for the service and then click **Go**. The address is queried and the services and operations that are available are listed.

3. In the **Namespace** dialog box, specify the namespace that you want to use: **AxCustomServicesRef**.

4. Click on the **Advanced** button available on this screen. The **Service Reference Settings** window opens.

Let's pause here and look at two options that are of particular interest to us – **Always generate message contracts** and **Collection type**.

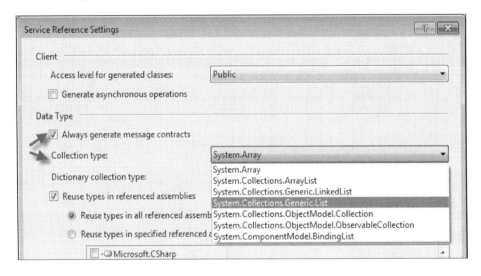

Always generate message contracts

The **Always generate message contracts** option determines if message contracts will be generated for the client. When you do not use this, the client has service operations that contain the same number of parameters as provided on the service operation. When this option is checked, message contracts are used on the service operations instead of the parameter list. The parameters that would normally be passed to the service operation are then wrapped in a message contract. This can be useful when you want to assure that all of the service operations take only one parameter.

If we look back at the previous sample code, this could also be modified to work with the message contracts that were generated, as demonstrated in the following code:

```
// Create the request message contract
CVRTitleServiceGetAllTitlesRequest theRequest = new CVRTitleServiceGet
AllTitlesRequest(theContext);

// Invoke the getAllTitles service operation
CVRTitleServiceGetAllTitlesResponse theResponse = theClient.
getAllTitles(theRequest);

// Retrieve the list of titles
CVRTitleListDataContract theListContract = theResponse.response;
```

Instead of just passing the context to the service operation, we need to create a request message contract. This contract is then passed to the service operation as the only parameter. All of the other parameters that you would use are contained in the message contract so that you can set them in the request message contract.

The service operation itself does not return the list in this case, but returns a response message contract. This response message contract itself contains the list.

Collection type

The collection type specifies the type of the collections that are used by the proxy client when dealing with collections. Though the service implementation uses a `List` as the collection type, you can choose to use arrays on the client side. This is the default option when creating a service reference. If we take a look back at the code that retrieves the list of titles, we can see that the resulting collection type is an array of `Title` objects.

```
// Invoke the getAllTitles service operation
CVRTitleListDataContract theListContract = theClient.getAllTitles(theContext);

// Loop all of the returned titles
foreach (Title title in theListContract.parmTitleList)
{
    Console.WriteLine(String.Format("{0}    Title[] CVRTitleListDataContract.parmTitleList    title.Description));
}
```

If we choose a different type, for example, `System.Collections.Generic.List`, we can see that the return type is now a generic list of `Title` objects instead of an array.

```
// Invoke the getAllTitles service operation
CVRTitleListDataContract theListContract = theClient.getAllTitles(theContext);

// Loop all of the returned titles
foreach (Title title in theListContract.parmTitleList)
{
    Console.WriteLine(String.Format("{0} System.Collections.Generic.List<Title> CVRTitleListDataContract.parmTitleList
}
```

Consuming the service

The following code uses the rental service and creates a rental with two titles. First, start by adding the using statement so that the types in the service reference are available to you. Use the following code to do this:

```
using DynamicsAxServices.Chapter4.Rentals.AxCustomServiceRef;
```

Then you can add the following code to consume the rental service:

```
CVRRentalCustomServiceClient client = new
CVRRentalCustomServiceClient();

// Create the rental header information
RentalHeader header = new RentalHeader();
header.MemberId = "M00001";
header.RentalId = "R00001";
header.ShopId = "S00002";
header.TransDate = DateTime.UtcNow;

// Create a rental line
RentalLine line = new RentalLine();
line.RentalId = "R00001";
line.Title = "T00001";
line.ReturnDate = DateTime.UtcNow;

// Create a second rental line
RentalLine secondLine = new RentalLine();
secondLine.RentalId = "R00001";
secondLine.Title = "T00003";
secondLine.ReturnDate = DateTime.UtcNow;

// Add it to the lines for the Rental
RentalLines lines = new RentalLines();
```

```
lines.LinesList = new List<RentalLine>();
lines.LinesList.Add(line);
lines.LinesList.Add(secondLine);

// Compose the Rental document
Rental Rental = new Rental();
Rental.RentalHeader = header;
Rental.RentalLines = lines;

// Invoke the creation of the Rental
long rentalRecId = client.createRental(null, Rental);


Console.WriteLine(String.Format("Rental created with record id {0}",
Convert.ToString(rentalRecId)));
Console.ReadLine();
```

To explain how it works, we will go through the code one block at a time. The first line of code is the following:

```
CVRRentalCustomServiceClient client = new
CVRRentalCustomServiceClient();
```

Just as in the previous samples, the first thing to do is to create an instance of the proxy client. When we have instantiated the client, we can start building the document that is required by the service operation that we are going to call. First up is the rental header.

```
RentalHeader header = new RentalHeader();
header.MemberId = "M00001";
header.RentalId = "R00001";
header.ShopId    = "S00002";
header.TransDate = DateTime.UtcNow;
```

The header is created by creating an instance of the RentalHeader contract. Note that this is a data contract that is generated by the SvcUtil tool and corresponds with CVRRentalHeaderDataContract. The name RentalHeader comes from the DataMemberAttribute attribute that we defined in X++.

```
RentalLine line = new RentalLine();
line.RentalId = "R00001";
line.Title = "T00001";
line.ReturnDate = DateTime.UtcNow;
```

The previous block of code creates a rental line. In this sample, we are adding two of those lines. As with `RentalHeader`, the same remark applies for the `RentalLine` type. This is the `CVRRentalLineDataContract` contract that has been generated at the client side with the name that was specified in the `DataMemberAttribute` attribute:

```
RentalLines lines = new RentalLines();
lines.LinesList = new List<RentalLine>();
lines.LinesList.Add(line);
lines.LinesList.Add(secondLine);
```

Next, the lines that we have created previously need to be added to a list data contract. We do this by creating an instance of the `CVRRentalLineListDataContract` contract. In this contract, we add a list containing the two lines that we have created:

```
Rental Rental = new Rental();
Rental.RentalHeader = header;
Rental.RentalLines = lines;
```

We have created the header, two lines, and a list containing these lines. At this point, we can glue these together and obtain a rental document object to pass to the service operation. The `Rental` type matches the `CVRRentalDocumentDataContract` contract and gets its name from the `DataMemberAttribute` attribute in X++.

```
long rentalRecId = client.createRental(null, Rental);

Console.WriteLine(String.Format("Rental created with record id
{0}",Convert.ToString(rentalRecId)));
```

Last but not least, we invoke the `createRental` service operation and pass the document to it. The result is `RecId` of the created `CVRRentalHeader` record.

Summary

It should be clear that custom services provide a fast and powerful way of exposing data and business logic. Custom services are capable of exposing both simple and complex entities. This makes them an alternative to document services. One aspect custom services are far superior in, is in exposing business logic. This will probably make custom services the preferred method of integration in many of your implementations.

In the next chapter, we will see how we can use custom service and data contracts in the `SysOperation` framework.

5
The SysOperation
Framework

The SysOperation framework is new in Microsoft Dynamics AX 2012, and is the preferred way of creating batch jobs. It replaces the RunBaseBatch framework, which remains available for backwards compatibility. When Microsoft Dynamics AX 2012 was released, the SysOperation framework was known as the Business Operation Framework or BOF.

The SysOperation framework provides all the functionality of the RunBaseBatch framework and more. In this chapter, we will discuss the differences between these frameworks, and point out the benefits of the SysOperation framework.

The following topics are covered in this chapter:

- **SysOperation versus RunBaseBatch**: In previous versions of Microsoft Dynamics AX, the RunBaseBatch framework was the preferred way of creating business logic that should run in batch. By comparing RunBaseBatch and SysOperation, we will show you that using SysOperation is the way to go in Microsoft Dynamics AX 2012.

- **Creating a SysOperation service**: We will demonstrate how to create a SysOperation service. Much of it will already be familiar to you as we will be using services and data contracts. Some new elements will be introduced, including attributes.

- **Running a SysOperation service**: The RunBaseBatch framework can only run logic in two modes: synchronously in the client or asynchronously in batch. The SysOperation framework has four modes; these modes are called execution modes. This section will help you in picking the best mode for your situation.

- **Custom controllers**: Some batches stand alone, but others are started in a specific context, for example a form. In many cases you want to act on the arguments this form passes to the SysOperation framework, such as the record that was selected. Creating custom controllers allows you to do so, and that's exactly what we will do.

- **Custom UI Builders**: When you want to modify the user interface of a SysOperation service, UI Builder classes are the way to go. In this part we will create a UI Builder class and look at the various ways we can change the behavior of the user interface.

- **Multithreading**: The SysOperation framework leverages the batch framework for better performance. It uses multiple threads that run in parallel to achieve a larger throughput.

At the end of this chapter, you will be able to create a SysOperation service, use controllers, and customize the user interface of a SysOperation service. You will also have learned how to improve the performance of your code using execution modes and runtime tasks.

SysOperation versus RunBaseBatch

Before going into the details on using the new SysOperation framework, let's put it next to the RunBaseBatch framework to find out what the main differences between the two of them are.

The first difference is that the SysOperation framework uses WCF services to run the processes and handle communication between the client and server. One of the advantages is that the client/server communication is less chatty so the connection doesn't need to be kept alive as opposed to the RPC communication of the RunBaseBatch framework.

The second big difference between the two is how they implement the Model-View-Controller (MVC) pattern. The RunBaseBatch framework uses one class that extends from the `RunBaseBatch` class. All of the components contained in the MVC pattern are contained within the same class.

- The **model** is identified by the **class members**.

- The **view** is handled by the `dialog`, `putToDialog`, and `getFromDialog` methods. These methods present a dialog to the user and help you to put data on and get data from the dialog.

- The **controller** is the **run method** as this is the place where you implement the business logic.

And with that said, the biggest disadvantage of the RunBaseBatch framework is clear: everything is contained in the same class.

The SysOperation framework makes better use of the MVC pattern than the RunBaseBatch framework does. All of the MVC components are separated.

- The **model** is handled by a class that defines the **data contract**.
- The **view** is a dialog that is now automatically generated by the **UI Builder**. This UI Builder uses the data contract to determine the contents of the dialog.
- The **controller** is being taken care of by the service controller class.

The implementation of the MVC pattern for both the frameworks is visualized in the following diagram:

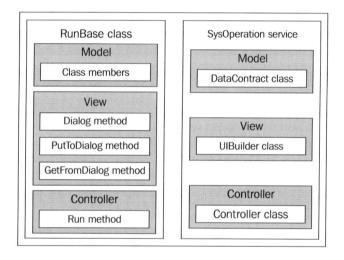

A third notable advantage is that it is fairly easy to expose SysOperation framework services to external consumers. The only thing that you need to do for this is add the SysOperation framework service to a service group and deploy this using an integration port.

So the advantages of the SysOperation framework can be summarized as follows:

- It makes use of services
- The SysOperation framework makes correct use of the MVC pattern
- More efficient client/server communication
- UI automatically generated based on data contracts
- Less extra effort in exposing the services externally
- It's a way to build service-oriented applications in Microsoft Dynamics AX

Creating a SysOperation service

In this demonstration, we will create a SysOperation service that detects members with overdue rentals. These members will get the status "blocked" by setting a checkbox on the member in the database.

The dialog for the service will look like the following screenshot:

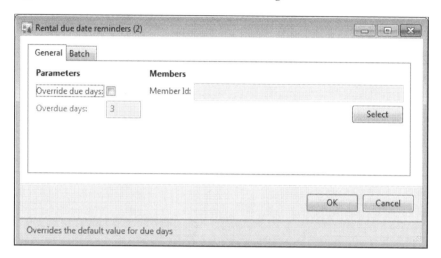

As you can see, a query enables you to select the members for which the rentals should be checked. By enabling the checkbox, you can override the number of overdue days that are allowed before a member is blocked.

The SysOperation framework uses services to execute business logic, so you have already learned most of the skills needed in *Chapter 4, Custom Services*.

Data contract

We will create a new data contract, but because we have already demonstrated the creation of a data contract in the earlier chapters, we can be briefer here. The data contract that we'll make will have three members:

- parmNumberOfOverdueDays: Holds the value for the number of overdue days that are allowed.

- parmOverrideNumOfDays: A Boolean that indicates that we want to override the number of overdue days allowed. We will use this later to demonstrate how to override the modifiedField method.

- parmQuery: Holds the query as a string.

Declaration and members

To start with, create a new class and name it CVRRentalDueDateReminderContract. Set the new method to protected and add a construct method in the same way as we did in the earlier examples. The rest of the class and its members look like the following code:

```
[DataContractAttribute]
public class CVRRentalDueDateReminderContract
{
    CVRNumberOverdueDays              numberOverdueDays;
    CVROverrideNumberOfOverdueDays   overrideNumOfDays;
    str                              packedQuery;
}

[DataMemberAttribute('OverdueDays'),
SysOperationDisplayOrderAttribute('2')]
public CVRNumberOverdueDays
parmNumberOverdueDays(CVRNumberOverdueDays _numberOverdueDays =
numberOverdueDays)
{
    ;
    numberOverdueDays = _numberOverdueDays;
    return numberOverdueDays;
}

[DataMemberAttribute('OverrideNumOfDays'),
SysOperationDisplayOrderAttribute('1')]
public CVROverrideNumberOfOverdueDays
parmOverrideNumOfDays(CVROverrideNumberOfOverdueDays
_overrideNumOfDays = overrideNumOfDays)
{
    ;
    overrideNumOfDays = _overrideNumOfDays;
    return overrideNumOfDays;
}

[DataMemberAttribute,
AifQueryTypeAttribute('_packedQuery', querystr(CVRMember))]
public str parmQuery(str _packedQuery = packedQuery)
{
    ;
    packedQuery = _packedQuery;
    return packedQuery;
}
```

As you can see, the data contract uses a number of new attributes. The `SysOperationDisplayOrderAttribute` attribute is used to specify the order in which the fields are displayed on the dialog. The `AifQueryTypeAttribute` attribute specifies that a member is a query. Adding this attribute will add a **Select** button and query values on the dialog.

Query helper methods

When we want to use a query on a SysOperation service, we have to declare it using a string variable in our data contract. You can clearly see this in the data contract we described previously. The data member must have the string type to make sure the data contract can be serialized.

To make working with the data contract easier, we will add two helper methods to the data contract. One method will set the query based on a query object, the other will return a query object based on the string value in the data contract.

```
public void setQuery(Query _query)
{
    packedQuery = SysOperationHelper::base64Encode(_query.pack());
}

public Query getQuery()
{
    return new Query(SysOperationHelper::base64Decode(packedQuery));
}
```

These methods are optional, but they make the code of other methods like the service operation cleaner.

Service and service operation

A SysOperation service needs a service and a service operation. This operation will be executed when the **OK** button is pressed on the dialog, or when the job executes in batch. Logically, this is where the business logic goes.

To create the service, add a new class to the AOT and name it `CVRRentalDueDateReminderService`:

```
public class CVRRentalDueDateReminderService
{
}
```

Next, add a new method. This method is the service operation and contains the business logic for the SysOperation service. The operation contains the following code:

```
[SysEntryPointAttribute(true)]
public void checkDueDates(CVRRentalDueDateReminderContract
_dueDateReminderContract)
{
    QueryRun      queryRun;
    CVRMember     cvrMember;
    ;

    // Get the query from the data contract
    queryRun = new QueryRun(_dueDateReminderContract.getQuery());

    // Loop all the members in the query
    while (queryRun.next())
    {
        // Get the current member record
        cvrMember = queryRun.get(tableNum(CVRMember));

        // Check if the member is already blocked
        if(!cvrMember.BlockedForRental &&
        this.doesMemberHaveOverdueRentals(cvrMember.RecId,
        _dueDateReminderContract.parmNumberOverdueDays()))
        {
            ttsBegin;
            cvrMember.selectForUpdate(true);
            cvrMember.BlockedForRental = NoYes::Yes;
            cvrMember.update();
            ttsCommit;
        }
    }
}
```

As you can see, a new QueryRun instance is created based on the query of the data contract. We use the helper method we added previously to retrieve the query object. Next, we use the queryRun object to loop all members, and check if the member has rentals that are overdue. If so, we set the BlockedForRental field to true on the member record.

The `doesMemberHaveOverdueRentals` method contains the logic that checks if the member has rentals that are overdue:

```
private boolean doesMemberHaveOverdueRentals(CVRMemberRefRecId
 _memberRecId, CVRNumberOverdueDays _overDueDays )
{
  CVRRentalTable   rentalTable;
  CVRRentalLine    rentalLine;
  TransDate        dateLimit = systemDateGet() - _overDueDays;
  ;

  // Check if there is a rental line that is not returned yet,
overdue and for the current member
  select firstOnly RecId from rentalLine
     join     RecId, Member from     rentalTable
     where    rentalTable.RecId   == rentalLine.Rental
     &&       rentalTable.Member  == _memberRecId
     &&       !rentalLine.ReturnDate
     &&       dateLimit > (rentalLine.DueDate);

  return rentalLine.RecId;
}
```

Menu item

The SysOperation framework is menu item-driven. To start a SysOperation service from the user interface, you click on a menu item. This menu item contains a few properties that are related to the SysOperation framework. We will discuss these properties in further detail later, but for now, let's just create a menu item in the most basic way. To create the menu item, perform the following steps:

1. In the developer workspace, open the AOT.

2. Expand the **Menu Items** node, then right-click on **Action** and click on **New Menu Item**.

3. Rename the menu item to `CVRRentalDueDateReminderService`.

4. Right-click on the menu item, then click on **Properties**.

5. Set the **Label** property to **Rental due date reminders**.

6. Set the **ObjectType** to **Class**, and enter `SysOperationServiceController` in the **Object** property.

7. In the **Parameters** field, enter `CVRRentalDueDateReminderService.checkDueDates`. This corresponds to the service class and service operation we want to use, seperated by a period.

8. Set the **EnumTypeParameter** property to **SysOperationExecutionMode** and the **EnumParameter** property to **Synchronous**.

9. Set the **RunOn** property to **Client**.

10. Right-click on the menu item, then click on **Save**.

Testing

Before testing, remember to compile CIL by clicking on the **Generate Incremental CIL** button or by pressing *Ctrl + Shift + F7*. When the compilation is successfully completed, you can run the SysOperation service. Just right-click on the **CVRRentalDueDateReminderService** menu item and click on **Open**. The following dialog will appear:

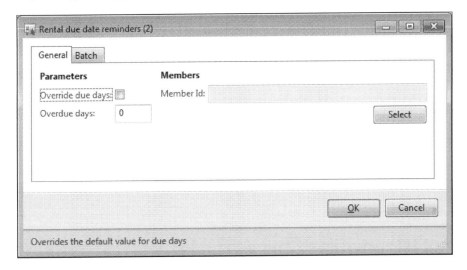

When the **OK** button is clicked, the service operation is executed using the parameters on the screen. You can open the CVRMember table to check that members with overdue rentals are blocked after the service has run.

Validation

When you create a SysOperation service, it is likely that you will need to validate the values that the user inputs. In our example, it would not make sense to allow the number of days to be an amount smaller than 1, because in that case the rental would not be overdue.

The SysOperation framework allows you to put validation code on the data contract. To enable this, the data contract should implement the SysOperationValidatable interface. The following is what the updated data contract looks like:

```
[DataContractAttribute]
public class CVRRentalDueDateReminderContract implements
SysOperationValidatable
{
    CVRNumberOverdueDays            numberOverdueDays;
    CVROverrideNumberOfOverdueDays  overrideNumOfDays;
    str                             packedQuery;
}
```

When you compile the data contract now, you should see one or more errors informing you that the class should implement the method validate. This is because we now implement an interface that has this method. So, add the following method:

```
public boolean validate()
{
  boolean ret = true;
  ;

  if (numberOverdueDays <= 0)
  {
    ret = checkFailed("The number of days overdue cannot be 0 or
    less");
  }

  return ret;
}
```

The method checks if the number of overdue days is smaller than or equal to 0, and if so, it returns false to indicate that the validation has failed.

Generate Incremental CIL and then run the service again. Enter 0 or less in the number of overdue days field, then click on **OK**, and you will see the following Infolog:

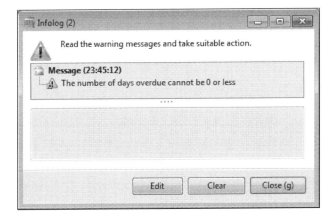

Defaulting

In our example, we also want the number of overdue days to get a default value that differs from 0, for example 3. The best way of doing this is by implementing the defaulting logic on the data contract. The data contract should implement the `SysOperationInitializable` interface to enable this:

```
[DataContractAttribute]
public class CVRRentalDueDateReminderContract implements
SysOperationValidatable, SysOperationInitializable
{
    CVRNumberOverdueDays            numberOverdueDays;
    CVROverrideNumberOfOverdueDays  overrideNumOfDays;
    str                             packedQuery;
}
```

Then add the `initialize` method and put the initialization code in it:

```
public void initialize()
{
    // default the number of overdue days to 3
    this.parmNumberOverdueDays(3);
}
```

Initialization will only occur the first time you open the dialog, from then on, usage data will be used. Before you test this, first remove your usage data. After that, generate Incremental CIL and then run the service again. You should see that the number of overdue days is defaulted to **3**:

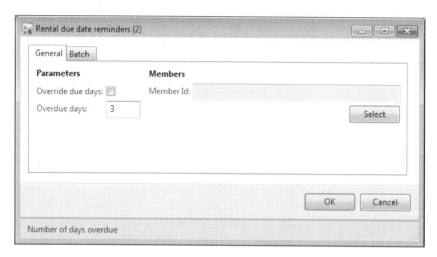

Running a SysOperation service

When a user has to be able to run a service by starting it in the user interface, the menu item becomes an important part of a SysOperation service. As we have seen earlier, the menu item has the following properties that the SysOperation framework needs:

- A **parameters** property that contains a reference to the service and service operation
- An **enum** parameter that determines the execution mode
- An **object** property where the controller that will be used is specified
- A **label** that will be displayed on the dialog

We will look at the first two properties now, and discuss the others later in this chapter.

Service and service operation

The menu item is linked to the service and service operation in the Parameters property. The format in which this parameter should be provided is `ServiceClass. ServiceOperation`, where `ServiceClass` is the name of the service class, and `ServiceOperation` is the name of the service operation, separated by a period.

Execution modes

The SysOperation framework allows both synchronous and asynchronous processing. In our example, we used synchronous processing by specifying the execution mode using the EnumTypeParameter and EnumParameter property. The EnumTypeParameter is set to SysOperationExecutionMode, which is a base enum that holds a value for each execution mode. The execution mode is specified in the EnumParameter property. There are four options to choose from:

- Synchronous
- Asynchronous
- ReliableAsynchronous
- ScheduledBatch

When the executing mode is not specified, ReliableAsynchronous will be used. To change the execution mode of our service, simply change the **EnumParameter** property on the **CVRRentalDueDateReminderService** menu item to the execution mode you want to use and run the service again. Let's look at what the results would be.

Synchronous

Synchronous execution of a SysOperation service has the same behavior as running a `RunBaseBatch` class. When you execute a SysOperation service synchronously, but not in batch, then the client will be unresponsive for the time it takes the operation to complete. All other execution modes are forms of asynchronous execution, including execution of a synchronous service in batch. When you enable the **Batch processing** checkbox on the **Batch** tab, then a batch job will be created, analogous to the behavior of `RunBaseBatch`.

Asynchronous

When a SysOperation service uses the asynchronous execution mode, the client will still be responsive while the operation executes. This is useful when you want a process to run in the background.

To run a service asynchronously, the service class must have an associated service node in the AOT. The service node has to be part of the AxClient service group, and the service group must be deployed again after the service is added to the group. If this isn't the case, the service will still run synchronously instead of asynchronously.

Reliable asynchronous

The reliable asynchronous execution mode differs from the regular asynchronous mode in that it creates a batch job. This ensures that the service will be executed completely, even if the client session in which it was started was destroyed, hence "reliable". The service will be visible among other scheduled batch jobs but, unlike these, it will be deleted when the execution has completed. It is still visible in the batch job history though.

The reliable asynchronous execution mode also differs from regular batches in that the user that executes the services will receive Infolog messages from the service when it has completed. This isn't the case with regular batches, where you need to check the log on the batch job manually.

Scheduled batch

The scheduled batch execution mode will schedule a batch job for the SysOperation service. Even when you don't check the **Batch processing** checkbox on the **Batch** tab of the service, it will still be executed in batch. On the same tab, you can set up the recurrence for the batch job. This will also be used even if the **Batch processing** checkbox isn't checked.

Custom controllers

In the earlier example, we used the `SysOperationServiceController` class on our menu item to run the services. This is the base controller, but you can create your own when you have the need. In this part, we will first take a look at some of the scenarios in which custom controllers can be used, after which we will create a custom controller.

Usage scenarios

What follows are two of the most common scenarios in which you would use a class that extends `SysOperationServiceController`. The first is using a controller to initialize a data contract, the second is a scenario in which you override methods of dialog fields.

Initializing the data contract

The controller can be used to initialize the data in the data contract. This is one of the most common scenarios in which a controller is used, and is the scenario we will demonstrate further on in this chapter. Initializing a data contract is usually done based on the `Args` object.

The `Args` object contains information such as:

- The execution mode
- The service operation that should be executed
- The menu item from which the controller is started
- The records that are selected when the menu item is executed
- The caller object

Dialog overrides

The dialog that is used by a SysOperation service is generated based on the `SysOperationTemplateForm` form, the data contracts, and the menu item. In most cases the default dialog that is generated is sufficient, but in other cases you'll want to customize the dialog. There are methods on the controller that allow you to do this. The following table lists the commonly used methods:

Method	Use
parmShowDialog	Set this to `false` if you want to avoid user interaction. The dialog will not be shown, yet the operation will still run.
parmDialogCaption	By default, the label of the menu item is used for the caption of the dialog. Use this method to override this.
caption	When a batch task is created, this label is used for its description. By default, it is the same as the `parmDialogCaption` method.
showQueryValues	When a query is used and this method returns `true`, then the fields with ranges and a **Select** button will be shown on the dialog. Return `false` in this method to hide them.
showQuerySelectButton	This method does the same as the `showQueryValues` method, but only affects the **Select** button.
canGoBatch	Return `false` in this method to hide the **Batch** tab.
templateForm	This method returns the form that the dialog is based on. By default, this is the `SysOperationTemplateForm` form, but you can override this method so that another form is used.
parmExecutionMode	You can either override or set this method before starting the operation to override the execution mode.

Obviously there are many other methods you can override, but discussing all of them would take far too long. When you override methods on the controller, always keep in mind that the controller is only part of your solution. Use it wisely and use the other components such as service operations, data contracts, and UI Builder classes where it is appropriate.

Study the code

The SysOperationServiceController class has a lot of documentation in its code that can help you figure out what the methods are for. You can also use the Type Hierarchy Browser to work out which classes extend the SysOperationServiceController class and get ideas from those.

Without further ado, let's see how we can create a controller for our example service.

Creating a controller

We want our controller to do the following things:

- Set a query range when the service is started from a form with a record selected

- Set the description of the batch tasks to reflect the record that is being processed

This is something we cannot accomplish with the SysOperationServiceController class, so we will have to create our own controller.

Declaration

To create a new controller, open the AOT and create a new class. Name it CVRRentalDueDateReminderController. Open the class in the X++ editor, and extend it from SysOperationServiceController. The classDeclaration should look like the following code:

```
public class CVRRentalDueDateReminderController extends
SysOperationServiceController
{
}
```

The main method

A controller is started by running a menu item. Because of this, it needs a `main` method, otherwise nothing will be executed. When creating a controller for your SysOperation service, the `main` method should be similar to the `main` method of the `SysOperationServiceController` class, shown as follows:

```
public static void main(Args args)
{
   SysOperationServiceController controller;

   controller = new SysOperationServiceController();
   controller.initializeFromArgs(args);
   controller.startOperation();
}
```

As you can see, a new controller is constructed, and is then initialized using the `args` object. This initialization will use the properties of the `args` object to get the execution mode and the service operation that needs to be executed. The controller is run using the `startOperation` method. You should always use this method to start an operation and refrain from using the `run` method.

We will create our `main` method slightly differently because we will put the `initializeFromArgs` call in a constructor, shown as follows:

```
public static void main(Args _args)
{
   CVRRentalDueDateReminderController
rentalDueDateReminderController;
   ;

   rentalDueDateReminderController =
CVRRentalDueDateReminderController::newFromArgs(_args);
   rentalDueDateReminderController.startOperation();
}

public static CVRRentalDueDateReminderController newFromArgs(Args
_args)
{
   CVRRentalDueDateReminderController
rentalDueDateReminderController;
   ;

     // Create a new instance of the controller
```

```
      rentalDueDateReminderController = new
CVRRentalDueDateReminderController();

   // Initialize from args
   // One of the things this will do is read the "parameters"
property from the menu item
   rentalDueDateReminderController.initializeFromArgs(_args);

   // Return a new instance of this controller
   return rentalDueDateReminderController;
}
```

As you can see, it's similar to the first `main` method and it paves the way for the additions we will make next.

Constructor

With the previous methods done, we basically have a custom controller that has the same functionality as the `SysOperationServiceController` class. We will extend the functionality of the `newFromArgs` method that we created so that the data contract is initialized. The final method will look like the following code:

```
public static CVRRentalDueDateReminderController newFromArgs(Args
_args)
{
   CVRRentalDueDateReminderController
rentalDueDateReminderController;
   CVRRentalDueDateReminderContract
rentalDueDateReminderContract;
   CVRMember                              member;
   Query                                  query;
   ;

   // Create a new instance of the controller
   rentalDueDateReminderController = new
CVRRentalDueDateReminderController();

   // Initialize from args
   // One of the things this will do is read the "parameters" property
from the menu item
   rentalDueDateReminderController.initializeFromArgs(_args);

   // Get the data contract
   // The string should be the same as the parameter name!
```

```
    rentalDueDateReminderContract =
rentalDueDateReminderController.getDataContractObject('_dueDateRem
inderContract');

  // Check if we are running this from a rental member
  if(_args && _args.dataset() == tableNum(CVRMember))
  {
    // Cast the record
    member = _args.record();

    // Create new query instance
    query = new query(queryStr(CVRMember));

    // Add a range on the member id
    query.dataSourceTable(tableNum(CVRMember)).addRange
(fieldNum(CVRMember, Id)).value(queryValue(member.Id));

    // Set the new query on the data contract
    rentalDueDateReminderContract.setQuery(query);

    // Notify the controller that we changed the query. This
avoids a refresh problem on the dialog
    rentalDueDateReminderController.queryChanged
('_dueDateReminderContract.parmQuery', query);
  }

  // Return a new instance of this controller
  return rentalDueDateReminderController;
}
```

As you can see, you can get the data contract instance using the
`getDataContractObject` method:

```
rentalDueDateReminderController.getDataContractObject('_dueDateRem
inderContract');
```

The string you pass as a parameter is the name of the data contract parameter of
the service operation that is used. It is very important to get this right. It can easily
be overlooked because the compiler does not check the validity of this parameter.

After that, it is simply a matter of setting parameter methods on the data contract.
When the service is started from the member form, we use the `Args` variable to set
a range on the query.

Menu item

The last thing we need to do is to create a menu item. To create a menu item, perform the following steps:

1. In the Development Workspace, open the AOT.

2. Expand the **Menu Items** node, then right-click on **Action** and click on **New Menu Item**.

3. Rename the menu item to CVRRentalDueDateReminderServiceCustomCon.

4. Right-click on the menu item, then click on **Properties**.

5. Set the **Label** property to **Rental due date reminders**.

6. Set the **ObjectType** to **Class**, and enter CVRRentalDueDateReminderController in the **Object** property.

7. In the **Parameters** field, enter CVRRentalDueDateReminderService. checkDueDates. This corresponds to the service class and the service operation we want to use.

8. Set the **EnumTypeParameter** property to **SysOperationExecutionMode**, and the **EnumParameter** property to **Synchronous**.

9. Set the **RunOn** property to **Client**.

10. Right-click on the menu item, then click on **Save**.

Testing

Before you start testing, remember to generate CIL by clicking the **Generate Incremental CIL** button or by pressing *Ctrl + Shift + F7*.

To test if the query range is added when the service is started from the members form, first add the menu item to the CVRMemberListPage form. When you click on the button that is created, you should see that the query range is added based on the record that was selected:

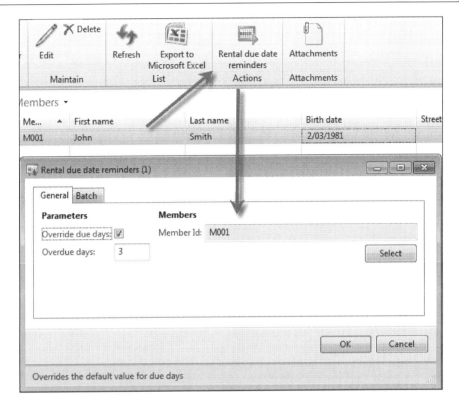

Custom UI Builders

One of the great improvements that the SysOperation framework has over the RunBaseBatch framework is that it generates the dialog for you. Fields on the dialog, for example, are generated based on the data contract. But if you want to change the dialog that is generated, you can use the UI Builder classes.

When we say custom UI Builders, we mean a class that extends the `SysOperationAutomaticUIBuilder` class. This is the class that generates the dialog based on the data contract of your service operation. By extending this class, you can add your own logic to the building process. Most commonly this will include logic that:

- Sets properties of field controls such as `mandatory` and `enabled`
- Overrides methods of field controls such as `lookup` and `modifiedField`
- Prevents controls from being added by overriding the `addDialogField` method

When you create your own UI Builder class, you will notice that the possibilities go far beyond what we have just described. Just as with the custom controllers, keep in mind that a UI Builder too is just a part of your solution. For example: when you feel that you are adding a lot of controls to your dialog using the UI Builder, consider using a template form on your controller instead. When you're putting a lot of validation code in your UI Builder, consider implementing the validation in the data contract in order to respect the MVC philosophy.

Creating a UI Builder

In this demonstration, we will create a UI Builder for our service. The purpose of this UI Builder is to override the `modifiedField` method of the checkbox control. It will behave in the following way:

- When the checkbox is checked, the control for the number of overdue days is enabled
- When the checkbox is blank, the control for the number of overdue days is disabled

Declaration

Let's start by creating the UI Builder class. Create a new class and name it `CVRRentalDueDateReminderUIBuilder`. This class will extend `SysOperationAutomaticUIBuilder`, as follows:

```
public class CVRRentalDueDateReminderUIBuilder extends
SysOperationAutomaticUIBuilder
{
    DialogField dialogFieldOverrideNumOfDays;
    DialogField dialogFieldNumberOfDueDays;

    CVRRentalDueDateReminderContract reminderContract;
}
```

Note that we have also declared three variables that we will use later:

- A dialog field for the checkbox
- A dialog field for the number of overdue days field
- A variable that holds the data contract

The override method

The first method we add is the method that will be executed when the value of the checkbox changes. This method will enable or disable the number of overdue days field. This is a very simple method that looks like the following code:

```
public boolean overrideNumOfDaysModified(FormCheckBoxControl
_checkBoxControl)
{
    ;
    // Enable or disable the number of days field based on the value
of the checkbox
    dialogFieldNumberOfDueDays.enabled(_checkBoxControl.value());

    return true;
}
```

As you can see, it uses the value of the `_checkBoxControl` parameter to set the `enabled` property of the control that holds the number of overdue days.

In this example, the parameter is of the type `FormCheckBoxControl` because we are overriding a method on a checkbox control. When you override a method on a control of a different type, you should use that type instead, for example `FormStringControl` for a string control. A full list of controls can be found in the system documentation. In the AOT, go to **System Documentation | Classes | FormControl**. Right-click on the **FormControl** node, then go to **Add-Ins | Type Hierarchy browser**. When you expand the **FormControl** node, you will see a list of all control types that are available. You can look these up in the system documentation to see what methods you can override.

The postBuild method

The `postBuild` method is called immediately after the dialog has been created, so it is a good place to put the logic that registers override methods. The code we need to add to this method is shown as follows:

```
public void postBuild()
{
    ;
    super();

    // Retrieve the data contract
    reminderContract = this.dataContractObject();

    // Retrieve the dialog fields
```

```
    dialogFieldOverrideNumOfDays =
this.bindInfo().getDialogField(reminderContract,
methodstr(CVRRentalDueDateReminderContract,
parmOverrideNumOfDays));
    dialogFieldNumberOfDueDays =
this.bindInfo().getDialogField(reminderContract,
methodstr(CVRRentalDueDateReminderContract,
parmNumberOverdueDays));

    // Register override methods
    dialogFieldOverrideNumOfDays.registerOverrideMethod
(methodstr(FormCheckBoxControl, modified),
methodstr(CVRRentalDueDateReminderUIBuilder,
overrideNumOfDaysModified), this);

    // Call the override already once to support packed value to be
sync immediately
    this.overrideNumOfDaysModified
(dialogFieldOverrideNumOfDays.control());
    }
```

Let's go through it step-by-step. The first line retrieves the data contract:

```
reminderContract = this.dataContractObject();
```

Next, we use the data contract together with the `bindInfo` object to get the controls for the checkbox and the number of overdue field:

```
dialogFieldOverrideNumOfDays =
this.bindInfo().getDialogField(reminderContract,
methodstr(CVRRentalDueDateReminderContract,
parmOverrideNumOfDays));
dialogFieldNumberOfDueDays =
this.bindInfo().getDialogField(reminderContract,
methodstr(CVRRentalDueDateReminderContract,
parmNumberOverdueDays));
```

In the previous code, the `bindInfo()` method returns an object of type `SysOperationUIBindInfo`. This contains information about which dialog controls the data members are bound to. By providing a reference to the `parmOverrideNumOfDays` and `parmNumberOverdueDays` members when calling the `getDialogField()` method, we get the dialog control that is associated with each member.

After we retrieve the dialog fields, we can register the override method. The following line does just that:

```
dialogFieldOverrideNumOfDays.registerOverrideMethod(methodstr(Form
CheckBoxControl, modified),
methodstr(CVRRentalDueDateReminderUIBuilder,
overrideNumOfDaysModified), this);
```

As you can see, we can use the `registerOverrideMethod()` method to override methods on the dialog fields. We simply point to the method we want to override (`FormCheckBoxControl.modified`), and the method that needs to be executed (`CVRRentalDueDateReminderUIBuilder.overrideNumOfDaysModified`).

Finally, we initialize the value of the `enabled` property by calling the override method directly. This will make sure that the checkbox reflects the values of the data contract after the dialog is built.

```
this.overrideNumOfDaysModified(dialogFieldOverrideNumOfDays.contro
l());
```

One more attribute

We have created a UI Builder class, but what remains is linking it to our data contract. That's what we use the `SysOperationContractProcessingAttribute` attribute for. To link the UI Builder class to the data contract, open the `CVRRentalDueDateReminderContract` class in the X++ editor, and add the `SysOperationContractProcessingAttribute` to it:

```
[DataContractAttribute
,SysOperationContractProcessingAttribute(classstr(CVRRentalDueDate
ReminderUIBuilder))]
public class CVRRentalDueDateReminderContract implements
SysOperationValidatable, SysOperationInitializable
{
    CVRNumberOverdueDays              numberOverdueDays;
    CVROverrideNumberOfOverdueDays   overrideNumOfDays;
    str                              packedQuery;
}
```

Testing

Now that you have added the UI Builder, you can test the service. But before you do, remember to generate CIL by clicking the **Generate Incremental CIL** button or pressing *Ctrl + Shift + F7*. When the CIL compilation is complete, right-click on the **CVRRentalDueDateReminderServiceCustomCon** menu item to open the dialog:

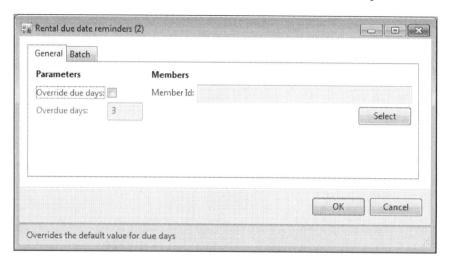

When you check the checkbox, you should see that the number of overdue days field is enabled. To disable the field, uncheck the checkbox.

Multithreading

Microsoft Dynamics AX 2012 has the ability to run jobs in batch by leveraging the abilities of the batch framework. The batch framework has two main purposes:

- Enable jobs to be scheduled.
- Provide a mechanism to split jobs up into smaller parts and run them in parallel. By doing so, the batch job has a larger throughput and the response time is much better.

We want the service that we created earlier to use the same batch framework so that it has better performance. There are different approaches to this and each has its advantages and disadvantages. The two most commonly used approaches can be described as:

- Individual task approach
- Helper approach

Individual task approach

This approach will divide the batch job into a number of work units also known as **runtime tasks**. For each work unit, a runtime task will be created. So you will have a one-to-one relation between work units and runtime tasks.

When your batch job is executing in batch, it is only responsible for creating the tasks for every unit of work to be done. Once the batch job is done creating tasks, it will be finished and the batch framework continues to work on the created runtime tasks in parallel.

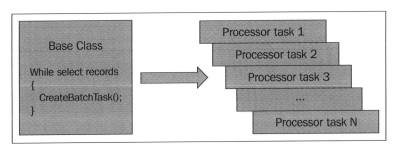

The advantages of using this approach are:

- Scales perfectly along with the schedule of the batch framework. It is possible to set up the batch framework to use a different number of threads depending on a time window during the day. The batch job will scale the number of threads depending on the number of threads set up for that time window and either use or yield resources.

- Assuming that your business logic is well designed, less effort is required to make your batch job multithread aware.

- You can easily create dependencies between the individual tasks.

The disadvantages of using this approach are:

- As some batch jobs may create a huge amount of tasks, there will be a lot of records in the batch framework's tables. This will have a negative impact on the performance as the framework needs to check dependencies and constraints before running each of the tasks.

- Though this approach is ideal to scale the schedule of the batch framework, you do not have control over the amount of threads processing your batch job on each of the batch servers. Once your task is assigned to a batch group picked up by an AOS, all of the free thread slots will be used for processing of your tasks.

Helper approach

The second approach that you can use to split up the work is by using **helpers**. Instead of creating an individual task for every unit of work to be done, we create a fixed number of threads. This resolves the issue we faced with the individual tasks where there were too many batch tasks being created in the batch framework tables.

Next to creating a fixed number of helper threads, we need to introduce a staging table to keep track of the work to be done. The helpers themselves look into this staging table to determine the next thing to be done when they have finished their current task.

The steps to follow when creating batch jobs that use this approach are as follows:

1. Create a staging table to contain the work list.
2. Create your batch job and let it be responsible for queuing the work in the staging table.
3. Build a worker class that can deal with the processing of one staging table record (contains business logic).
4. Create a helper class that is able to pick the next task and call the worker.
5. Add code to the batch job to spawn helper threads until the desired number of helpers are available.

As for the staging table, you need to provide the following fields in the staging table:

- An identifier field
- A reference field that may point to a record or contain information that helps the workers to know what needs to be done
- A status field to keep track of what's done and what needs to be done

Also keep in mind that helpers must use pessimistic locking to retrieve the records from the staging table. This is to make sure that two helper threads do not select the same record and start working on the same task.

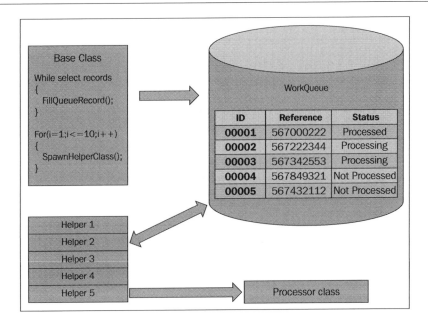

The advantages of using this approach are:

- You have control over how many threads are processing your batch job. This can be useful when you want your tasks to leave threads open on the AOS for other batch jobs when scaling the number of threads available for batch processing on the AOS instance.

- The batch tables are not filled with a huge number of tasks as only a fixed number of helper threads are created. This lowers the performance hit when checking dependencies and constraints.

- If you put a little effort into a generic solution for this approach, you can re-use the same staging table for different batch jobs.

The disadvantages of using this approach are:

- Because the number of threads is fixed, this approach does not scale as well as the individual task approach. Scaling up the number of threads on the AOS servers will not result in more working threads and higher throughput.

- It is slightly more work to create the staging table needed for the helper threads to keep track of the work to be done than it is to spawn runtime tasks.

- This approach is not suitable to process a huge number of small tasks as maintaining the staging table would have a negative influence on the performance and throughput.

Useful link

If you want to learn more about these two approaches, you can find a series of blog posts on this topic on the MSDN blog of the Dynamics AX Performance Team. The first blog post of the series can be found at http://blogs.msdn.com/b/axperf/archive/2012/02/24/batch-parallelism-in-ax-part-i.aspx.

Enabling multithreading

Now that we know the differences between these approaches, we can go ahead and update our SysOperation service to provide multithreading support. Because implementing both approaches would take too long, we will use the individual task approach only. Firstly, we have to extend our service class from the SysOperationServiceBase class. The declaration should look like the following code:

```
public class CVRRentalDueDateReminderService extends
SysOperationServiceBase
{
}
```

This is needed because the SysOperatonServiceBase class contains methods that allow us to work with the batch header and check whether the code is running in batch.

Next, we add a new operation to our service. The operation differs from the existing one because it does not do the work itself. Instead it creates runtime tasks that do the work. The full code listing is as follows:

```
[SysEntryPointAttribute(true)]
public void checkDueDatesMulti(CVRRentalDueDateReminderContract
_dueDateReminderContract)
{
   QueryRun      queryRun;
   CVRMember     cvrMember;

   BatchHeader                            batchHeader;
   SysOperationServiceController          runTaskController;
   CVRRentalDueDateReminderContract       runTaskContract;
   Query                                  taskQuery;
      ;

   // Get the query from the data contract
   queryRun = new QueryRun(_dueDateReminderContract.getQuery());
```

```
  // Loop all the members in the query
  while (queryRun.next())
  {
    // Get the current member record
    cvrMember = queryRun.get(tableNum(CVRMember));

    // Create new controller for the runtime task
    runTaskController = new SysOperationServiceController
(classStr(CVRRentalDueDateReminderService),
methodStr(CVRRentalDueDateReminderService, checkDueDates));

    // Get a data contract for the controller
    runTaskContract = runTaskController.getDataContractObject
('_dueDateReminderContract');

    // create query for task
    taskQuery = new Query(queryStr(CVRMember));
    taskQuery.dataSourceTable(tableNum(CVRMember)).
addRange(fieldNum(CVRMember, Id)).value(cvrMember.Id);

    // set variables for the data contract
    runTaskContract.setQuery(taskQuery);
    runTaskContract.parmNumberOverdueDays
(_dueDateReminderContract.parmNumberOverdueDays());

    // If running in batch
    if(this.isExecutingInBatch())
    {
      // If we do not have a batch header yet
      if(!batchHeader)
      {
        // Get one
        batchHeader = this.getCurrentBatchHeader();
      }

      // Create a runtime task
      batchHeader.addRuntimeTask(runTaskController,
this.getCurrentBatchTask().RecId);
    }
    else
    {
      // Not in batch, just run the controller here
      runTaskController.run();
    }
  }
```

```
    // After all of the runtime tasks are created, save the
batchheader
    if(batchHeader)
    {
        // Saving the header will create the batch records and add
dependencies where needed
        batchHeader.save();
    }
}
```

Let us break up the code and take a look at it piece by piece. The top part of the method remains roughly the same just up to the query part. We still get the query from the data contract and loop all of the results.

```
// Get the query from the data contract
queryRun = new QueryRun(_dueDateReminderContract.getQuery());

// Loop all the members in the query
while (queryRun.next())
{
    // Get the current member record
    cvrMember = queryRun.get(tableNum(CVRMember));
```

What follows is more interesting. Instead of running our business logic, we create a controller for the runtime task and point to the `checkDueDates` method. In this example, we have chosen to re-use the same data contract and service operation that we created earlier to act as the runtime task.

```
    runTaskController = new SysOperationServiceController
(classStr(CVRRentalDueDateReminderService),
methodStr(CVRRentalDueDateReminderService, checkDueDates));

    // Get a data contract for the controller
    runTaskContract = runTaskController.
getDataContractObject('_dueDateReminderContract');
```

After creating a controller, a data contract is constructed to pass to the runtime task. We re-use the same contract that is also used by the job service. Because of that, we need to create a query object that contains a range on the member's `Id` field.

```
    // Get a data contract for the controller
    runTaskContract = runTaskController.
getDataContractObject('_dueDateReminderContract');

    // create query for task
    taskQuery = new Query(queryStr(CVRMember));
```

```
    taskQuery.dataSourceTable(tableNum(CVRMember)).addRange
(fieldNum(CVRMember, Id)).value(cvrMember.Id);

    // set variables for the data contract
    runTaskContract.setQuery(taskQuery);
    runTaskContract.parmNumberOverdueDays
(_dueDateReminderContract.parmNumberOverdueDays());
```

What follows is the part that will create the runtime tasks. First a batch header instance is constructed if we do not have one already. The batch header class is used to contain the information on runtime tasks that we add to the running batch job. Once the batch header class is instructed to save that information, the actual records are created in the batch table along with all of the dependencies.

```
    // If running in batch
    if(this.isExecutingInBatch())
    {
      // If we do not have a batch header yet
      if(!batchHeader)
      {
        // Get one
        batchHeader = this.getCurrentBatchHeader();
      }

      // Create a runtime task
      batchHeader.addRuntimeTask(runTaskController,
this.getCurrentBatchTask().RecId);
    }
    else
    {
      // Not in batch, just run the controller here
      runTaskController.run();
    }

    // After all of the runtime tasks are created, save the
batchheader
    if(batchHeader)
    {
      // Saving the header will create the batch records and add
dependencies where needed
      batchHeader.save();
    }
```

Summary

It should be clear that the SysOperation framework is not only a replacement for the RunBaseBatch framework, it also improves upon it. Many of the improvements are due to the implementation of the MVC pattern. This allows for re-use of many of the components such as the data contracts, service operations, and controllers.

Reusing these components enables batch processing for existing services, and rapid development of new services. More than that, the different execution modes allow these services to run synchronously and asynchronously with little effort by developers. It is even possible to leverage the power of the batch framework to run processes in parallel, all in a way that is scalable. This improves the overall performance and user experience.

Up until now, we have always created services in Microsoft Dynamics AX and exposed them to external applications. In the next chapter, we will reverse the roles and consume an external service in Microsoft Dynamics AX 2012.

6
Web Services

For the better part of this book, we have developed services in Microsoft Dynamics AX and exposed them. But in this chapter, we will show how to consume a web service from Microsoft Dynamics AX 2012.

In previous versions of Microsoft Dynamics AX, you could add a web service reference in a reference node in the AOT. This generated proxy classes and other artifacts you could then use to consume the service. In Microsoft Dynamics AX 2012, there is no longer an option to add a service reference to the AOT. Instead Microsoft Visual Studio is used to generate all artifacts, which are then added to the AOT.

How this works and how this can be done will all become clear in this chapter.

The following topics will be covered in this chapter:

- **Installing prerequisites**: Because part of the development takes place in Visual Studio, we have to install additional components. You will learn what components to install and what they do.

- **Visual Studio development**: After introducing the demo service, we will create a reference to the service with the aid of Visual Studio. We will take you through this process step-by-step.

- **X++ development**: Finally, we will demonstrate how we can use the Visual Studio project to consume the service in Microsoft Dynamics AX. You will also gain insight into the different deployment modes that are available to deploy the project's output.

Installing the Visual Studio Tools

Part of the coding that is needed to consume an external service is done in Visual Studio. That is why we must install both Visual Studio 2010 and the Visual Studio Tools for Microsoft Dynamics AX 2012 before we can create Visual Studio projects and add them to the AOT.

To do this, follow these steps:

1. Run the Microsoft Dynamics AX 2012 setup.
2. Go to the **Install** section and choose **Microsoft Dynamics AX Components**.
3. Click on the **Next** button to move to the next screen and choose **Add or modify existing components**.
4. Look under the **Developer Tools** node and select **Visual Studio Tools**.
5. Go through the rest of the setup wizard to complete the installation process.

Installing **Visual Studio Tools** will add the following extensions to Visual Studio:

- The **Application Explorer** option that is available in Visual Studio under **View | Application Explorer**. Enabling it will display the AOT in Visual Studio.

- Two new templates that are available when you create a new project in Visual Studio—**Report Model** and **EP Web Applications**.

- An option to add Visual Studio projects to the AOT. This is the option we're interested in when consuming web services.

Visual Studio development

When consuming a service, the first thing you need to do is create a reference to the service. Since this can no longer be done in Microsoft Dynamics AX, we have to use Visual Studio. So, we'll do that, but first we'll examine the service we are going to consume.

Introducing the USA zip code service

To show you how Microsoft Dynamics AX 2012 enables developers to consume web services, we are going to use an example zip code service. This service is available on the website of RESTful web services.

What is a RESTful web service?

REST stands for **Representational State Transfer** and it represents a set of design principles by which web services are developed. For more details about REST, you can go to `http://www.ibm.com/developerworks/webservices/library/ws-restful/`.

You can find lots of other example services on the website of RESTful web services at `http://www.restfulwebservices.net/servicecategory.aspx`. When creating references to the services available there, always remember to use the WCF version of the service you want to use.

In the zip code service, we have two operations available to use when referencing the WCF version; these are as follows:

- `GetPostCodeDetailByPostCode`: This operation takes a zip code a parameter and returns a `PostalCode` data contract with all of the information about the `PostalCode` info we searched for.

- `GetPostCodeDetailByPlaceName`: This operation takes place names as parameters and also returns a `PostalCode` data contract with the needed information.

Creating the Visual Studio proxy library

In Microsoft Dynamics AX 2012, Visual Studio projects can be contained in the AOT. This enables us to use Visual Studio to create a class library project and add it to the AOT. The advantage is that Visual Studio deals with the service reference. It uses the `SvcUtil` tool to create the proxy client and generate the types needed to consume the service.

Perform the following steps to create a Visual Studio class library project:

1. In Visual Studio, select **File | New | Project**.
2. In the **New Project** window, select **Visual C#** and select the **Class Library** project type.

3. In the **Name** textbox, give the project a name and click **OK**. These steps are illustrated in the following screenshot:

Adding the service reference

Next, we will create a service reference to the USA zip code service. To do this, follow these steps:

1. Locate the **References** node in the project.

2. Right-click on the **References** node and select **Add Service Reference….** The **Add Service Reference** window opens.

3. In the **Address** drop-down box, specify the following address for the service: **http://www.restfulwebservices.net/wcf/USAZipCodeService.svc?wsdl** and then press **Go**. The address is queried and the two operations mentioned above are listed.

4. In the **Namespace** dialog box, specify the namespace that you want to use: **USAZipCodeServiceRef**. The **Add Service Reference** window should look like this:

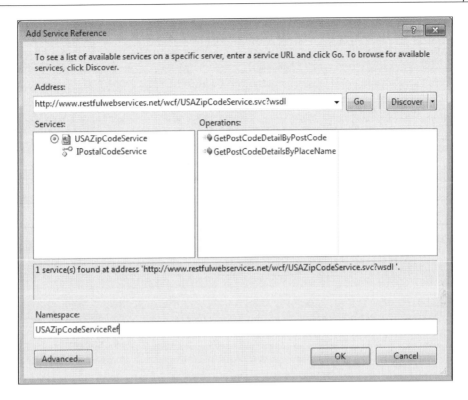

5. Click **OK**. The service will be added to the **Service References** node.

6. Delete the `Class1.cs` class, as we will not need it.

7. To add the project to the AOT, right-click the project, then click **Add RestfulServiceNet.PostalService** to the AOT.

8. After the project has been added to the AOT, you can specify the deployment options. In the properties of the project, set **Deploy to Client** and **Deploy to Server** to **Yes**.

9. Finally, right-click the project and click **Deploy**.

X++ development

The Visual Studio project and its output have been added to the AOT, so the first stage of development is now complete. You can leave Visual Studio and turn back to Microsoft Dynamics AX 2012. The project has been added to the **Visual Studio Projects** node in the AOT. Because we have used C#, the project will be in the **C Sharp Projects** node.

Look for the **DynamicsAxServices.WebServices.ZipCode** project and expand some of the nodes to inspect it. It should look like this:

As you can see, this is divided into the following two main components:

- The **Project Content** node contains the actual C# project source, such as properties of the project, the service references, an `app.config` file, and C# source files

- The **Project Output** node contains the assemblies that will be deployed, taking into account the deployment options.

In order to use the assemblies that have been created and are stored in the AOT, we'll have to deploy them. Let's look at the options that are available.

Managed code deployment

When we create a project in Visual Studio and add it to the AOT, the following deployment options are available:

- **Deploy to Client**
- **Deploy to Server**
- **Deploy to EP**

In our example earlier, we have enabled deployment on the client and to server, because these are important in the context of services.

Deploy to Server

When you have enabled deployment to server, the output of the Visual Studio project will be copied to the `VSAssemblies` subfolder in the bin folder of the AOS. The default path is `C:\Program Files\Microsoft Dynamics AX\60\Server\<AOSServer>\Bin\VSAssemblies`. After you have deployed assemblies to the server, you should restart the AOS so that they are loaded.

Hot swapping

When hot swapping is enabled on the AOS, no restart is needed after
deployment. This feature is added for the convenience of developers,
but is not recommended for a production environment. For more info,
check the following article on MSDN: **How to: Enable Hot Swapping
of Assemblies** (http://msdn.microsoft.com/en-us/library/
gg889279.aspx).

Deploy to Client

When you have enabled deployment to client, then the output of the Visual Studio
project will be copied to the following folder on the client: `%localappdata%\
Microsoft\Dynamics Ax\VSAssemblies`. You may have to restart the Microsoft
Dynamics AX client after deployment, otherwise the assemblies may not be copied.

The assemblies will be deployed to a client as they are needed. This comes down to
the following three situations:

- When you use IntelliSense
- When you compile code that uses the assembly
- When code runs on the client in which a call is made to the assembly

Obviously, as a developer you will want to have the assembly on your client,
otherwise you will not be able to use IntelliSense or compile your code.

Consuming the web service

Now that we have created a service reference in our Visual Studio proxy library
and deployed it to Microsoft Dynamics AX, we can use the types in the library
from within Microsoft Dynamics AX.

First attempt

Let us take a look at the X++ code that consumes the zip code service to retrieve
a place name. To do just that, we have the following code:

```
static void Consume_GetZipCodePlaceName(Args _args)
{
  DynamicsAxServices.WebServices.ZipCode.USAZipCodeServiceRef.
PostalCodeServiceClientpostalServiceClient;
  DynamicsAxServices.WebServices.ZipCode.USAZipCodeServiceRef.
PostalCodepostalCode;
```

```
    System.ExceptionException;
    ;

    try
    {
      // Create a service client proxy
      postalServiceClient = new DynamicsAxServices.WebServices.ZipCode.
USAZipCodeServiceRef.PostalCodeServiceClient();

      // Use the zipcode to find a place name
      postalCode= postalServiceClient.
GetPostCodeDetailByPostCode("10001"); // 10001 is New York

      // Use the getAnyTypeForObject to marshal the System.String to an
Ax anyType
      // so that it can be used with info()
      info(strFmt('%1', CLRInterop::getAnyTypeForObject(postalCode.get_
PlaceName())));
    }
    catch
    {
      // Get the .NET Type Exception
      exception = CLRInterop::getLastException();

      // Go through the inner exceptions
      while(exception)
      {
        // Print the exception to the infolog
        info(CLRInterop::getAnyTypeForObject(exception.ToString()));

        // Get the inner exception for more details
        exception = exception.get_InnerException();
      }
    }
  }
}
```

When we go through the code bit by bit, we can see that a proxy client is created first. Note that this is the managed type created by the SvcUtil tool when adding the service reference.

```
postalServiceClient = new DynamicsAxServices.WebServices.ZipCode.
USAZipCodeServiceRef.PostalCodeServiceClient();
```

After that, using the following code we immediately invoke the service operation with a zip code:

```
postalCode= postalServiceClient.GetPostCodeDetailByPostCode("10001");
// 10001 is New York
```

Then, there is a simple infolog message showing the place name.

```
info(strFmt('%1', CLRInterop::getAnyTypeForObject(postalCode.get_
PlaceName())));
```

Notice the `CLRInterop::getAnyTypeForObject` method, which is used to marshal between the .NET type `System.String` and the X++ `anyType` type before submitting it to the infolog.

That's it for consuming the service. But we also have some exception handling going on in there to handle any .NET exceptions while invoking the external service, as shown in the following code snippet:

```
catch
{
  // Get the .NET Type Exception
  exception = CLRInterop::getLastException();

  // Go through the inner exceptions
  while(exception)
  {
    // Print the exception to the infolog
    info(CLRInterop::getAnyTypeForObject(exception.ToString()));

    // Get the inner exception for more details
    exception = exception.get_InnerException();
  }
}
```

Fixing configuration issues

Although the previous example code should suffice, you will get an error message when running it. The error message is shown in the following screenshot:

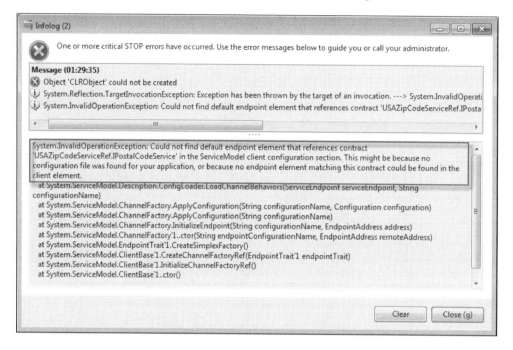

What is going on here is that the service is trying to look for the endpoint configuration in the application's configuration file, but doesn't seem to find it. This is because Microsoft Dynamics AX is acting as the host application here (Ax32.exe). Therefore, the service tries to open the Ax32.exe.config file and look for the endpoint configuration.

It is clear that putting the configuration details of every service that we want to consume into the Ax32.exe.config file is a bit impractical and should be avoided. The solution to this issue is using the AifUtil class to create the service client.

Let us change the previous code so that it uses the AifUtil class to point to the right configuration file and see what happens then. Start off by declaring a new variable of the type System.Type at the top of the job, as shown here:

```
System.Type type;
```

Then replace the following line of code:

```
postalServiceClient = new DynamicsAxServices.WebServices.ZipCode.
USAZipCodeServiceRef.PostalCodeServiceClient();
```

With the following two lines of code that use the variable you just declared:

```
type= CLRInterop::getType('DynamicsAxServices.WebServices.ZipCode.
USAZipCodeServiceRef.PostalCodeServiceClient');
postalServiceClient = AifUtil::createServiceClient(type);
```

The first line will resolve the .NET type of the service client and pass it to the `AifUtil::createServiceClient` method. The `AifUtil` class will then resolve the right configuration file by looking into the `VSAssemblies` folder for the assembly that contains the specified type. You can see the code of the `AifUtil` class' `screateServiceClient` method in the following code snippet:

```
vsAssembliesPath = xApplication::getVSAssembliesPath();

configFilePath = Microsoft.Dynamics.IntegrationFramework.ServiceRefere
nce::GetConfigFilePath(serviceClientType, vsAssembliesPath);

serviceClient = Microsoft.Dynamics.IntegrationFramework.ServiceReferen
ce::CreateServiceClient(serviceClientType, configFilePath);
```

When you test these changes, the service should be called correctly and give an infolog message showing **New York** as the place name.

Deploying between environments

Although the previous code consumes the external service just fine, there is another impractical issue going on when you want to deploy the code across environments.

Suppose that you want to have different versions of your service running on development, test, and production systems. Then you will probably have three different addresses for each environment. But the issue here is that you only have one address available in the proxy class library.

To solve this issue, we need to update our X++ code one more time. Start by declaring two new variables that will hold the endpoint and endpoint address:

```
System.ServiceModel.Description.ServiceEndpointendPoint;
System.ServiceModel.EndpointAddresssendPointAddress;
```

You may have to add a reference to the `System.ServiceModel` assembly to the AOT. To do that, go to the AOT, right-click on the **References** node, and then click **Add Reference**. Next, select **System.ServiceModel** in the grid, click **Select**, and finally **OK**.

Then add the following three lines of code just before the line that invokes the service operation:

```
endPointAddress = new System.ServiceModel.EndpointAddress("http://www.
restfulwebservices.net/wcf/USAZipCodeService.svc");

endPoint = postalServiceClient.get_Endpoint();

endPoint.set_Address(endPointAddress);
```

What the preceding code does is create an endpoint address for the service client to use. When the endpoint is created, it replaces the endpoint address currently used by the service client. Note that in the previous example, the address should be replaced by a parameter stored in the system. That way you can set the endpoint address depending on the parameter value of that environment.

Final result

After all these changes, the code that consumes the services looks like this:

```
static void Consume_GetZipCodePlaceNameWithEndPoint(Args _args)
{
  DynamicsAxServices.WebServices.ZipCode.USAZipCodeServiceRef.
PostalCodeServiceClient postalServiceClient;
  DynamicsAxServices.WebServices.ZipCode.USAZipCodeServiceRef.
PostalCodepostalCode;
  System.ServiceModel.Description.ServiceEndpointendPoint;
  System.ServiceModel.EndpointAddressendPointAddress;
  System.Exceptionexception;
  System.Typetype;
  ;

  try
  {
    // Get the .NET type of the client proxy
    type = CLRInterop::getType('DynamicsAxServices.WebServices.
ZipCode.USAZipCodeServiceRef.PostalCodeServiceClient');

    // Let AifUtil create the proxy client because it uses the
VSAssemblies path for the config file
    postalServiceClient = AifUtil::createServiceClient(type);

    // Create and endpoint address, This should be a parameter stored
in the system
```

```
        endPointAddress = new System.ServiceModel.EndpointAddress
("http://www.restfulwebservices.net/wcf/USAZipCodeService.svc");

        // Get the WCF endpoint
        endPoint = postalServiceClient.get_Endpoint();

        // Set the endpoint address.
        endPoint.set_Address(endPointAddress);

        // Use the zipcode to find a place name
        postalCode = postalServiceClient.
GetPostCodeDetailByPostCode("10001"); // 10001 is New York

        // Use the getAnyTypeForObject to marshal the System.String to an
Ax anyType
        // so that it can be used with info()
        info(strFmt('%1', CLRInterop::getAnyTypeForObject(postalCode.get_
PlaceName()))));
    }
    catch(Exception::CLRError)
    {
        // Get the .NET Type Exception
          exception = CLRInterop::getLastException();

        // Go through the inner exceptions
        while(exception)
        {
          // Print the exception to the infolog
          info(CLRInterop::getAnyTypeForObject(exception.ToString()));

          // Get the inner exception for more details
          exception = exception.get_InnerException();
        }
    }
}
```

Summary

At first sight the procedure to consume a service in Microsoft Dynamics AX 2012 might seem a bit complex, but once you've done it you see how easy it really is. By using Visual Studio you can take advantage of having control over how you create the reference. You can choose whether you want to use message contracts, re-use data types, and so on.

Support for different deployment options also means that it is easier than ever to use managed code. The assemblies are part of the model store and are deployed when needed, so no manual actions are needed to deploy them.

In the next chapter, we will take a closer look at the system services that are available. They are new to Microsoft Dynamics AX, so they are easily overlooked when planning for integration. Because of their flexibility, it is worth considering using them.

7
System Services

With each new release of Microsoft Dynamics AX, new features for developers are added. These range from wizards that are used to automate certain repetitive development tasks to support for new technologies such as WCF. From a developer's perspective you might think that Microsoft is really generous to provide us with all these cool features. This is true to a certain extent, but providing developers with tools can never be an end goal. In reality, these features are added to facilitate new functionality in Microsoft Dynamics AX.

This is also true for a new set of services that are supported in Microsoft Dynamics AX 2012 known as system services. These services are WCF services that allow you to access system information. For example, they are used in the Excel add-in.

This doesn't mean you can't use them in your solutions. On the contrary, in this chapter we will demonstrate how you can use these services to build your applications.

The following topics will be covered in this chapter:

- **System services**: We will start with a general description of the three types of system services along with the introduction of the demo application we will build.

- **Metadata service**: The first service we will use is the metadata service, a service that exposes information about the AOT. We will discuss what information can be retrieved and how it can be done.

- **Query service**: Next, we will look at the query service, a service that, as the name suggests, allows you to execute queries on the Microsoft Dynamics AX database and retrieve the results.

- **User session service**: We will conclude with an explanation of the user session service, a service that allows you to obtain user session-related information.

What are system services?

System services are automatically installed when the Application Object Server is installed and are available when the AOS instance is running. They are written by Microsoft in managed code and hence they cannot be customized.

As mentioned, there are three system services, as follows:

- Metadata service
- Query service
- User session service

We will have a detailed discussion of these later in the chapter. We will not be able to go into every detail of all service operations, but it will be more than enough to get you started. Fortunately, for those who want to dig deeper, these services are well documented on MSDN.

A demo application

To demonstrate the usage of the different system services, we start with a demo application. The application is a Windows Forms application that contains the following elements:

- A combobox containing the **Contoso Video Rental** queries
- A DataGridView control to contain the resulting data
- **Previous page** and **Next page** buttons to provide paging of the result
- A ListBox control containing session information of the calling user

The design of the demo application is shown in the following screenshot:

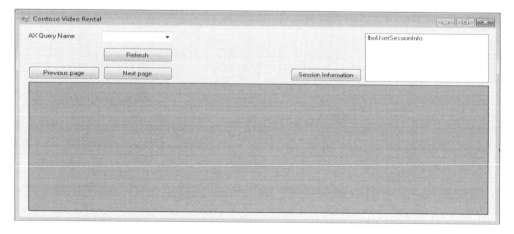

The following Microsoft Dynamics AX services are used in the application and for each of them a service reference is created:

- **Metadata service**: `http://DYNAX01:8101/DynamicsAx/Services/MetaDataService`
- **Query service**: `http://DYNAX01:8101/DynamicsAx/Services/QueryService`
- **User session service**: `http://DYNAX01:8101/DynamicsAx/Services/UserSessionService`

When creating the references, you should replace **DYNAX01** with the name of the server on which your AOS is installed, and specify the correct port to use, which is **8101** by default. All of the service references we use in the demonstration have been configured to use the `System.Collections.Generic.List` collection type.

Metadata service

The metadata service allows external consumers to obtain information about the AOT objects within Microsoft Dynamics AX, such as tables, queries, forms, and so on. When we take a look at the operations available on the service, we can see the following two types of operations:

- Operations that return a list of object names, such as the `GetQueryNames` operation which returns a list of query names available in the system
- Operations that return metadata of one particular object to the consumer, such as the `GetTableMetaData` operation which takes a list of table names and returns all of the metadata information available for these tables

> You can find detailed class diagrams on MSDN describing the metadata classes at `http://msdn.microsoft.com/en-us/library/gg845212`.

Filling the combobox

Let's start by taking a look at the code that is executed when the form loads.

To fill the combobox, we need to use the `GetQueryNames` operation on the metadata service and filter the results to show only the queries that start with CVR. You can use the following code to do this:

```
private void MainForm_Load(object sender, EventArgs e)
{
    // Create a service client
```

```
AxMetadataServiceClient client = new AxMetadataServiceClient();

// Get queries from Ax that start with CVR
IList<string> queryNames = client.GetQueryNames()    .Where(queryItem
=> queryItem.StartsWith("CVR")).ToList();

// Set the results as the combobox's data source
cboAxQueryName.DataSource = queryNames;
}
```

First, the service client is created:

```
AxMetadataServiceClient client = new AxMetadataServiceClient();
```

Next, the following line invokes the operation to retrieve all of the query names. We apply a little lambda expression to the IList object to filter out the queries that start with CVR by using the following line:

```
IList<string> queryNames = client.GetQueryNames()    .Where(queryItem
=> queryItem.StartsWith("CVR")).ToList();
```

Lastly, we just take the result and set it as the data source of the combobox by using the following line of code

```
cboAxQueryName.DataSource = queryNames;
```

When running your application, you should see the following result:

Query service

The query service enables us to retrieve data from Microsoft Dynamics AX without having to use the .NET Business Connector or, even worse, access the SQL database directly.

By using the query service, you can fetch data using any of the following query types:

- **Static query**: This is used to retrieve data by using queries that are present in the AOT. We will use this type in the demonstration.

- **User-defined query**: A query can also be created by using the `QueryMetadata` class. By doing this, you can create a query in the same way as you create queries in X++ code.

- **Dynamic query**: Another way of running a query is by creating an X++ class that extends the `AifQueryBuilder` class. You can invoke the `ExecuteQuery` operation by passing in the name of the query builder class. It is also possible to pass arguments by using a class that extends from the `AifQueryBuilderArgs` class.

Fetching data for the grid

Now let's put some code behind the clicked event handler of the **Refresh** button. The idea is to invoke the query service to retrieve the data of the selected query and put it into the DataGridView control.

Put the following code behind the **Refresh** button's clicked event handler to get the job done:

```
private void cmdRefresh_Click(object sender, EventArgs e)
{
  this.refreshData();
}
```

Before this can work, we obviously need to add a `refreshData` method that does the refreshing part. This is put in a separate method to support re-use of the code when we add paging later on:

```
private void refreshData()
{
  try
  {
    // Determine the selected query / datamember
    string dataMember = cboAxQueryName.Text;
    string queryName = cboAxQueryName.Text;

    // Create a binding source for members
    BindingSource bindingSource = new BindingSource();
```

```
        // Set the binding source as the data source for the data grid
        dtgAxData.DataSource = bindingSource;

        // Create a service client
        QueryServiceClient queryClient = new QueryServiceClient();

        // Create an empty paging object
        Paging paging = null;

        // Call the query to retrieve the results
        DataSet dataSet = queryClient.ExecuteStaticQuery(queryName,
    ref paging);

        // Set as the data source of the binding source
        bindingSource.DataSource = dataSet;
        bindingSource.DataMember = dataMember;
    }
    catch (Exception _ex)
    {
        MessageBox.Show(_ex.Message);
    }
}
```

The first two lines of code set the chosen query name and the data member. This data member is the actual list that is bound to the binding source. Here, we have the same name as the query because the **CVRMember** table has the same name as the **CVRMember** query object, as shown in the following code:

```
// Determine the selected query / datamember
string dataMember = cboAxQueryName.Text;
string queryName = cboAxQueryName.Text;
```

Next, the binding source is created and set as the data source of the DataGridView control:

```
// Create a binding source for members
BindingSource bindingSource = new BindingSource();

// Set the binding source as the data source for the data grid
dtgAxData.DataSource = bindingSource;
```

Now we can start to think about fetching data from Microsoft Dynamics AX. So let's create a service client and call the operation to execute the query. Note that for now we have a variable of type `Paging` that is set to `null` because we add paging functionality later in this chapter.

```
// Create a service client
QueryServiceClient queryClient = new QueryServiceClient();

// Create an empty paging object
Paging paging = null;

// Call the query to retrieve the results
DataSet dataSet = queryClient.ExecuteStaticQuery(queryName, ref
paging);
```

Once the dataset containing the resulting records is returned, we can set it as the data source for the binding source.

```
// Set as the data source of the binding source
bindingSource.DataSource = dataSet;
bindingSource.DataMember = dataMember;
```

That's all there is to it. To test the code, run the application and hit the **Refresh** button with the **CVRMember** query selected. The result should look like this:

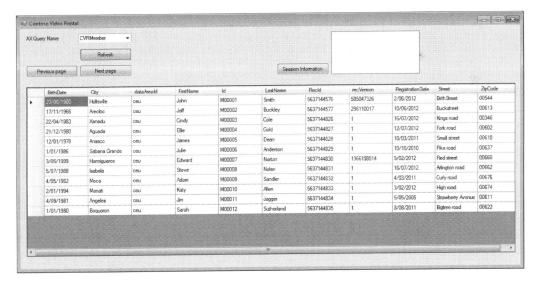

Paging the results

The next thing that we want to enable in our application is paging. To handle large data sets we can make use of paging to retrieve only a defined number of records at a time. In our example, we want to use pages of ten records.

The first thing to do is to add a member variable to the form that keeps track of the starting position:

```
private int nextStartPosition = 1;
```

The code behind the paging buttons is rather simple and will just decrement or increment the starting position for data retrieval by 10. After adjusting the starting position, data is refreshed by calling the refreshData method as seen before:

```
private void cmdNextPage_Click(object sender, EventArgs e)
{
    nextStartPosition += 10;
    this.refreshData();
}
private void cmdPreviousPage_Click(object sender, EventArgs e)
{
    nextStartPosition -= 10;
    this.refreshData();
}
```

The code behind the paging buttons is in place, but we still need to add some code to the refreshData method to actually deal with the paging of the data. So we need to replace the following line of code:

```
// Create an empty paging object
Paging paging = null;
```

Replace it with the following piece of code that tells the query service to only fetch 10 records starting from the currently calculated starting position:

```
// Create a paging object to start at the starting offset and fetch 10
records
Paging paging = new PositionBasedPaging()
{
    NumberOfRecordsToFetch = 10,
    StartingPosition = nextStartPosition
};
```

When we now run our application, the result should be as shown in the following screenshot:

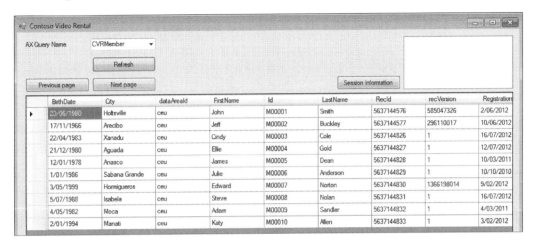

Notice that we only have ten records in our DataGridView control and by clicking the **Next page** button we get to see the next set of records, as shown in the following screenshot:

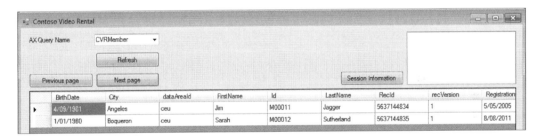

 For paging techniques like position-based paging to work, you have to use a query that contains a sorting field. This field will be used to order the results before the paging is applied.

User session service

The last system service that we will discuss is the user session service. This service exposes information about the current user and its session. Although this service is categorized by Microsoft as a system service, technically it isn't. Unlike other system services, the business logic is contained in a service class in the AOT and exposed using a basic port. Consequently, it is also possible to expose this service using an enhanced port, allowing you to further customize the service.

The user session has the following operations:

- GetUserSessionInfo: This returns information about the current session in the form of an instance of the UserSessionInfo class containing the following information: language, currency, company, company time zone, user-preferred time zone, preferred calendar, user ID, whether the user is a system admin, and the locale name.

- GetAccessRights: Returns a collection of the type AccessRight that contains the permissions that the user has on the items that were provided as parameters such as tables, fields, and menu items.

- ApplyTimeZone: Executes the DateTimeUtil::applyTimeZoneOffset method and thereby offsets the utcdatetime value by the amount specified in the timezone parameter.

- RemoveTimeZone: Executes the DateTimeUtil::removeTimeZoneOffset method and thereby removes the offset specified by the timezone parameter from the utcdatetime value.

We will use the GetUserSessionInfo and GetAccesRights operations in the following scenario to demonstrate how to use this service.

Retrieving user information

The functionalities that we will add to the form are as follows:

- A button is added to retrieve the user session information
- A ListBox control is added to display the user session information
- General user information is retrieved such as the company and language
- Permissions are retrieved for the query data source

To enable this functionality, override the cmdUserSessionInfo_Click method using the following code:

```
private void cmdUserSessionInfo_Click(object sender, EventArgs e)
{
    // Create an instance of the usersession client
    UserSessionServiceClient client = new UserSessionServiceClient();

    // Get session information
    UserSessionInfo sessionInfo = client.GetUserSessionInfo(null);

    // Put all of the information in the listbox
    lboUserSessionInfo.Items.Clear();
```

```
    lboUserSessionInfo.Items.Add("User : " + sessionInfo.UserId);
    lboUserSessionInfo.Items.Add("Company : " + sessionInfo.Company);
    lboUserSessionInfo.Items.Add("Language : " + sessionInfo.
AXLanguage);
    lboUserSessionInfo.Items.Add("Currency : " + sessionInfo.
CurrencyInfo.CurrencyCode);
    lboUserSessionInfo.Items.Add("Administrator : " + sessionInfo.
IsSysAdmin);

    // Create a access control item for the main table of the selected
query
    AccessControlledItemKey key = new AccessControlledItemKey()
    {
      ItemType = AccessControlledType.Table,
      ItemName = cboAxQueryName.Text
    };

    // Create a list with the item in it
    List<AccessControlledItemKey> keys =
new List<AccessControlledItemKey>();
    keys.Add(key);

    // Now request the effective access right for this user session on
the item
    List<AccessRight> accessRights = client.GetAccessRights(null, keys);

    // Get the access rights
    AccessRight accessRight = accessRights.First();

    lboUserSessionInfo.Items.Add("Query access right : " + accessRight.
ToString());
    }
```

As you can see, we can divide the code into the following two large parts:

- First, we use the `GetUserSessionInfo` operation to retrieve the session information, and use it to add items to the listbox.

- Next, we create a new list object of type `AccessControlledItemKey` and add an item specifying the table name. Then we use the `GetAccessRights` method to retrieve the permissions that the user has on this table and add them to the list.

To test the code, simply click the **Session Information** button and the listbox should be filled with the session information, as shown in the following screenshot:

Summary

System services are new in this iteration of Microsoft Dynamics AX, but they are spot on. In this chapter, we have demonstrated that system services are powerful, especially when they are used together.

If you use system services where possible, you're using out-of-the-box functionality that Microsoft Dynamics AX 2012 offers. This will save you the time that you would spend developing document or custom services, thereby allowing you to focus on more important tasks.

Index

I

K

M

N

O

OperationContract attribute **36**
operation contracts **23**
operations, service classes
  about **55**
  create **55**
  delete **55**
  find **56**
  findkeys **56**
  GetChangedKeys **56**
  GetKeys **56**
  read **56**
  update **56**
operations, user session service
  ApplyTimeZone **166**
  GetAccessRights **166**
  GetUserSessionInfo **166**
  RemoveTimeZone **166**
outbound integration ports **12**
outbound ports **23, 24**

P

parmDialogCaption method **123**
parmExecutionMode method **123**
parmNumberOfOverdueDays **112**
parmOverrideNumOfDays **112**
parmQuery **112**
parmShowDialog method **123**
pipelines **8**
pipelines, enhanced ports
  about **29**
  value substitution **30**
  XSL **30**
prepareForSave method **50, 51**

Q

query, document service
  creating **58**
query helper methods **114**
QueryRun instance **115**
query service
  about **16, 160**
  data, fetching for grid **161, 162**
  query types **161**

results, paging **164**
  URL **159**
query types, query service
  dynamic query **161**
  static query **161**
  user-defined query **161**

R

ReadList method **55**
Read operation **73, 75**
registerOverrideMethod() method **133**
reliable asynchronous execution mode **122**
RemoveTimeZone operation **166**
rental data contracts
  about **99**
  CVRRentalDocumentDataContract **100**
  CVRRentalDocumentListDataContract **100**
  CVRRentalHeaderDataContract **99**
  CVRRentalLineDataContract **99**
  CVRRentalLineListDataContract **99**
  diagrammatic representation **99**
rental header **98, 108**
rental registering, custom service example
  about **103**
  Always generate message contracts
      option **105**
  collection type **105, 106**
  message contracts, generating **105**
  service, consuming **106-108**
  service reference, creating **104**
rental service, custom services deployment
  about **98**
  createRental service operation **100, 101**
  line tables **98**
  rental data contracts **99, 100**
  rental header **98**
  service operations **98**
rental service operations
  about **98**
  CreateRental **98**
  GetAllRentals **99**
  GetAllRentalsForMember **99**
Representational State Transfer. *See* REST
request preprocessor **8**
response postprocessor **8**

REST 145
results, query service
  paging 164
runtime tasks 135

S

scheduled batch execution mode 122
security, enhanced ports 31
serialization 87
serializeClass method 50
serializeDocument method 49
service class
  about 55, 90
  operations 55
service contract, document service
  updating 65
service contracts 16, 23, 90
service deployment
  about 23
  basic, versus enhanced ports 24
  inbound, versus outbound ports 24
  service operations 24
service generation
  about 35
  CIL 40
  generated artifacts 35
  service contract definition 36
  service contract, implementing 36, 37
  WCF configuration storage 38, 39
service group 25
service node 56
service operations 24
service operations, enhanced ports 28
service reference
  adding, to USA zip code service 146
services
  about 6
  complexity, handling 18
  custom service 15, 16
  document services 15
  flexibility 18
  selecting 17
  system services 16
  types 14
  user session service 17

service types
  selecting 18
setLineNum method 54
showQuerySelectButton method 123
showQueryValues method 123
SOA
  about 6
  architecture overview 7, 8
  example implementations 6
SOAP 37
static query 161
SvcUtil tool 107
synchronous execution mode 121
SysEntryPointAttribute 89
SysObsoleteAttribute 88
SysOperation framework
  about 14, 109
  advantages 14, 109, 111
  versus, RunBaseBatch 110
SysOperation service
  creating 112
  data contract, creating 112
  defaulting 119
  enum parameter 120
  execution modes 121
  menu item 116
  parameters property 120
  running 120
  service and service operation 114, 115, 120
  testing 117
  validation 117, 118
SysOperationServiceController 122
SysOperatonServiceBase class 138
system services
  about 16, 158
  demo application 158, 159
  metadata service 17, 159
  query service 16, 160
  user session service 17, 165

T

tasks troubleshooting, document service
  about 63
  constraints 64
  labels 64

Thank you for buying
Microsoft Dynamics AX 2012 Services

About Packt Publishing

Packt, pronounced 'packed', published its first book "Mastering phpMyAdmin for Effective MySQL Management" in April 2004 and subsequently continued to specialize in publishing highly focused books on specific technologies and solutions.

Our books and publications share the experiences of your fellow IT professionals in adapting and customizing today's systems, applications, and frameworks. Our solution based books give you the knowledge and power to customize the software and technologies you're using to get the job done. Packt books are more specific and less general than the IT books you have seen in the past. Our unique business model allows us to bring you more focused information, giving you more of what you need to know, and less of what you don't.

Packt is a modern, yet unique publishing company, which focuses on producing quality, cutting-edge books for communities of developers, administrators, and newbies alike. For more information, please visit our website: www.packtpub.com.

About Packt Enterprise

In 2010, Packt launched two new brands, Packt Enterprise and Packt Open Source, in order to continue its focus on specialization. This book is part of the Packt Enterprise brand, home to books published on enterprise software – software created by major vendors, including (but not limited to) IBM, Microsoft and Oracle, often for use in other corporations. Its titles will offer information relevant to a range of users of this software, including administrators, developers, architects, and end users.

Writing for Packt

We welcome all inquiries from people who are interested in authoring. Book proposals should be sent to author@packtpub.com. If your book idea is still at an early stage and you would like to discuss it first before writing a formal book proposal, contact us; one of our commissioning editors will get in touch with you.

We're not just looking for published authors; if you have strong technical skills but no writing experience, our experienced editors can help you develop a writing career, or simply get some additional reward for your expertise.

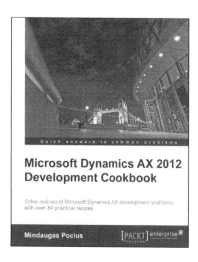

Microsoft Dynamics AX 2012 Development Cookbook

Solve real-world Microsoft Dynamics AX development problems with over 80 practical recipes

Mindaugas Pocius

Microsoft Dynamics AX 2012 Development Cookbook

ISBN: 978-1-84968-464-4   Paperback: 372 pages

Solve real-world Microsoft Dynamics AX development problems with over 80 practical recipes

1. Develop powerful, successful Dynamics AX projects with efficient X++ code with this book and eBook.

2. Proven recipes that can be re-used in numerous successful Dynamics AX projects.

3. Covers general ledger, accounts payable, accounts receivable, project modules and general functionality of Dynamics AX.

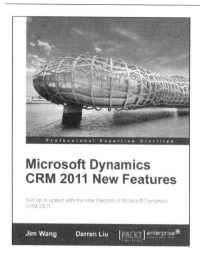

Microsoft Dynamics CRM 2011 New Features

Get up to speed with the new features of Microsoft Dynamics CRM 2011

Jim Wang   Darren Liu

Microsoft Dynamics CRM 2011 New Features

ISBN: 978-1-84968-206-0   Paperback: 288 pages

Get up to speed with the new features of Microsoft Dynamics CRM 2011

1. Master the new features of Microsoft Dynamics 2011.

2. Use client-side programming to perform data validation, automation, and process enhancement.

3. Learn powerful event driven server-side programming methods: Plug-Ins and Processes (Formerly Workflows).

4. Extend Microsoft Dynamics CRM 2011 in the Cloud.

Please check **www.PacktPub.com** for information on our titles

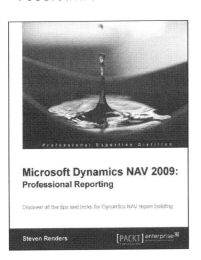

26346152R00106

Made in the USA
Lexington, KY
03 October 2013